Sept

A Gift of love [   ] P9-DHA-691
your day — mom

The Honey Cookbook

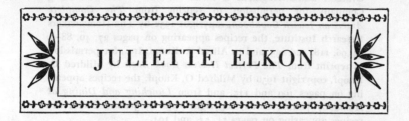

JULIETTE ELKON

The Honey Cookbook

ALFRED A KNOPF   NEW YORK   1975

Grateful acknowledgment is made to The World Publishing Company for permission to reprint from *The Complete American-Jewish Cookbook,* copyright 1952 by The Homemakers Research Institute, the recipes appearing on pages 27, 40, 88–9, 93, 96, 118, and 135, and to Alfred A. Knopf, Inc., for permission to reprint from *The Perfect Hostess Cook Book* by Mildred O. Knopf, copyright 1950 by Mildred O. Knopf, the recipes appearing on pages 109 and 115, and from *Lunching and Dining at Home* by Jeanne Owen, copyright 1942 by Jeanne Owen, the recipes appearing on pages 51, 54, and 104.

L. C. catalog card number: 55–9283

© Juliette Elkon, 1955

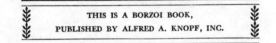

THIS IS A BORZOI BOOK,
PUBLISHED BY ALFRED A. KNOPF, INC.

Published October 24, 1955
Printed Four Times
Sixth Printing, March 1975

Preface

*T*HIS is the first general book of honey recipes to be published. Honey is, of course, at its best in cakes, cookies, and candies, and a large portion of recipes in this book is devoted to baking and desserts. But honey can be used to advantage in almost any kind of cooking that would ordinarily call for sugar. To many, the use of honey in meat and vegetable recipes may seem odd, but I believe that if you try some of these recipes the result of your efforts will seem very worth while.

Honey is a fascinating substance to work with. It adds an unmistakable flavor and blends well with other ingredients. Despite its apparent stickiness it makes beautifully smooth doughs when mixed with flour and cereals; bowls and hands come out clean, almost waxy.

My research into ancient honey cookery has shown that many of the best-known recipes were in use earlier than A.D. 1600. But from the middle of the seventeenth century until early in this one, honey had not been used very widely. Manuscripts of the Renaissance speak of a great shortage of honey. The beehives had been ruined and fell into neglect because of the endless wars that decimated Europe and the continual shifts of population in search of security.

Sugar cane, native to China and imported to the Middle East about 300 B.C., was introduced to Europe by the Crusaders in the thirteenth century. Princely households alone could afford the new luxury of manufactured sugar. In due time, and with the usual competitive spirit, it became every housewife's ambition to try the new sweet. As the manufacture of sugar grew, no one remembered it had been made as a substitute for honey.

Today scientists searching for the prolongation of life have again brought bees and honey into the limelight. Some of the claims of early physicians who considered honey a miraculous healing substance are being re-evaluated and may to some extent be vindicated.

We know enough to say that from the point of view of health honey is more valuable than sugar. It relieves a very common desire for sweets without creating sugar addiction, a rising urge which may change metabolism and produce illness.

As a monosaccharide—or simple sugar—honey requires no digestive changes before assimilation and provides the quickest source of energy in the diet of growing children. Bacteria cannot live in honey. Therefore it is a safe and wholesome food.

Recent research at the University of Chicago has shown that honey has a beneficial influence on the retention of calcium by infants. It also contains a considerable amount of minerals, B vitamin complex, amino acids, and enzymes.

It is, however, to your sense of taste in particular that I wish to appeal in presenting these recipes. I have deciphered and toned down mediæval dishes to our modern palates; I have experimented with new combinations and tested the results several times. My choice is in no way absolute, and I recommend personal exploration. I believe, however, that you will find in these recipes a comprehensive guide to new and better enjoyment of the finest natural sweet, and that such enjoyment will be beneficial to your health.

Acknowledgments

I WISH to thank Mr. William Cole for his editorial assist-
ance, and Mr. Lawrence M. Clum for his suggestions and cor-
rections.

Thanks are also due Miss Harriet M. Grace, Director of the
American Honey Institute, Madison, Wisconsin, for her per-
mission to use certain recipes perfected by the American Honey
Institute, and to Alfred Roth, President of the New Rochelle
Beekeepers Association, for his kindly co-operation.

Purchase, New York
March 27, 1955

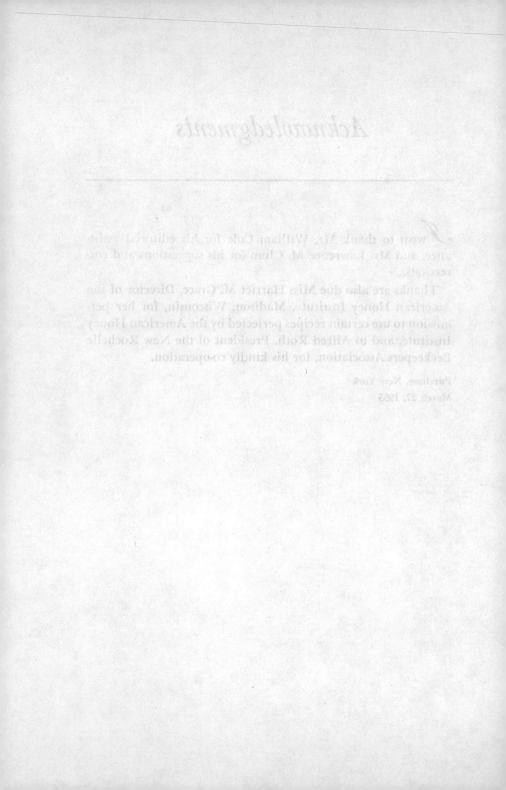

Contents

ALL ABOUT HONEY 3

OF CEREALS, PANCAKES, AND WAFFLES 8

OF HORS D'OEUVRES, ENTREES, AND VEGETABLES 18

OF CUSTARDS, PUDDINGS, AND PIES 59

OF CAKES, COOKIES, AND FROSTING 78

OF CANDY, CARAMELS, AND PRALINES 138

OF MEAD, PUNCH, AND COCKTAILS 148

The Honey Cookbook

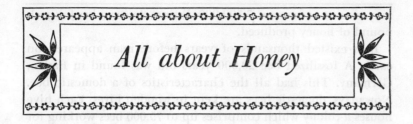

All about Honey

$\mathcal{W}$HEN ready for fertilization, most flowers collect an accumulation of soluble sugars at their base. These sugars, called nectar, act as a quick food supply to nourish the newly formed seed after fertilization. Being powerfully fragrant, nectar attracts some insects, particularly bees, which will, while gathering their food, brush the male pollen on the female organ of the flower, an action called pollination. Bees are aware of the specific time when this flower secretion occurs.

It is a scientifically accepted fact that bees communicate with one another: their buzzing varies in intensity, and their bodies sway in specific directions signaling to the other bees the distance to the source of the nectar and the point of the compass at which it can be found. The nectar from each flower has its individual flavor, a fact which bees recognize. They will often forsake nearby flowers and travel several miles to gather nectar from flowers more to their taste.

Not all cultivated flowers yield nectar, and some of the most beautiful ones, like Japanese cherry blossoms, roses, and certain varieties of iris, are valueless to the bees. Watching bees in my garden I find they most often prefer clovers, wild flowers, and aromatic herbs. I have seeded these in all available spaces.

The nectar, when transformed by the enzyme of special glands in the bodies of the bees and evaporated by the fanning of their wings, is called honey. The bees make honey for their own use, as their main food. Visiting flower after flower, they may contact as many as 7,500,000 distinct flower tubes for each pound of honey produced.

Bees existed thousands of years before man appeared on earth. A fossilized bee 20,000 years old was found in Baden, Germany. This had all the characteristics of a domestic bee. Nowadays, domestic bees are kept in wooden hives. Each hive houses a colony which comprises up to 75,000 bees working for the queen bee. Until recently, naturalists assumed that relations between the queen and her subjects were governed by instinct. But Dr. Colin Butler, doing entomological research at the Hampshire experimental station in Britain, found that worker bees show such remarkable devotion to their queen simply because her abdomen is covered with a tasty sweet substance. This substance can be rubbed off the queen's body with a cotton wad which afterwards is as attractive to bees as their queen. However, as soon as she becomes ill or grows old, the substance dries up and the workers start to build cells for another queen.

A queen's duty is to lay eggs. As a virgin she lays unfertilized eggs and these hatch as drones—or male bees—thus insuring her own fertilization in nuptial flight. Only the strongest, the most perfect drone, will be able to fly to the dizzying height the queen reaches in the one flight she takes away from the hive. After mating, the drone will die, leaving a supply of sperm within the queen's body. Upon her return to the hive she settles down and daily lays her weight in eggs until she dies. These eggs become sterile female workers, nurses, or guards. But regardless of how many eggs the queen lays, the nurse bees regulate the population of the hive, killing any larvæ above the number that the food supply will nourish. The nurses can make a new queen by enlarging a cell and feeding that particular larva a special diet.

Drones and workers who can't produce their quota of honey are thrown out to die of exposure. Walking among the flowers in my garden I often find bees between petals, their mandibles

close to the pistil, their wings worn with miles and miles of
flying, their small pollen sacs like a yellow velvet button on
their legs—seemingly asleep, but lifeless, in a fitting shroud.

All bees go through four stages of growth: egg, larva, pupa,
and adult. It takes 72 hours for the eggs to hatch, 21 days for
workers to come to maturity, 24 days for drones to do the
same. But the queen, who gets a special diet, is fully developed
after 16 days.

Royal jelly, a milky-white substance, is fed to all larvæ for
three days by the nurse bees. It is fed to the queen throughout
her long life—3 to 7 years, compared with 2 to 6 months for
other bees. Royal jelly is rich in protein, pantothentic acid,
amino acids, and various vitamins. Adapted for human use it
may become a factor in the prolongation of life. In the last
few years scientists of France, Germany, Mexico, Canada, and
the United States have been probing the mystery of this jelly
to test its therapeutic value for man.

The art of beekeeping, or apiculture, developed slowly. In
the early stages of civilization bees were wild and made hives
in any suitable cavities. Wild bees may still be found in the
remoter parts of the world, as in Africa, where pale-green
honey drips from gigantic red combs. Early man killed the
bees to get at the honey. The domestication of bees in man-
made hives began in Asia and along the Mediterranean shores
four thousand years before Christ. The Egyptians, the Greeks,
and the Romans were quite adept at it. Virgil, who used to
help his father tend the hives on his farm near Mantua, said
much about bees that the modern apiarist will corroborate.
However, believing, like most Romans, in masculine suprem-
acy, he called the ruler of the hive the "king bee."

In other parts of the world, forest or log apiary was prac-
ticed. Cavities twelve to twenty feet above the ground were
dug out of living trees. The hollows were rubbed with thyme
and melissa, or other sweet-smelling herbs, and painted with a
little honey. A captured swarm was released into each hollow

and soon settled there. The individual, family, or tribe who owned the swarm marked the tree.

At first, honey was eaten mostly out of the comb. T. M. Davis, an American explorer, found the oldest jar of honey, in a perfect state of preservation, in the tomb of Queen Tyi's parents in Egypt, where it had been placed over 3000 years ago.

Today, in the United States, there are more than 400,000 beekeepers, and honey production is rising. The demand is such that it still has to be supplemented heavily with imports from France, Mexico, Israel, Malta, and Iraq.

Made from the nectar of more than eighteen hundred species of plants, trees, and shrubs, honeys from different regions of the United States vary greatly in flavor, color, and consistency. When standing for some time, all honeys will show dextrose crystals starting to accumulate at the bottom of the jar. The speed with which this precipitation takes place depends on the source of the nectar. This process is called granulation. Speedy granulation produces very fine crystals. The false notion that granulating honey is spoiling, which is all too prevalent in the United States, has led certain packers to heat and strain their honey to such an extent that it will not form crystals. This processing, called pasteurizing, robs honey of most of the properties which make it a unique food. Signs of granulation are a guarantee of non-pasteurized, and therefore of high-quality, honey.

Most brand-name honeys are blends of differently flavored honey from various sources. Standardization is obtained by heating slightly and mixing them all together until the desired flavor is obtained. The flavor and texture of "farm-type" honey, which is often bottled by the beekeeper himself, varies from season to season, depending on the selection of nectar made by the bees. The "farm-type" honey is seldom pasteurized.

A good fluid honey must have a high degree of viscosity, or

stickiness—the proof that it is fully ripened and will not fer-
ment. When the jar is turned over, a large air bubble will rise
from the cap to the bottom. The slower it moves, the richer
the honey.

Honey should be stored at room temperature. Refrigeration
will hasten granulation. Granulated honey can be restored to
liquid form by immersing the jar in a hot (not boiling) water
bath until the crystals disappear.

Of Cereals, Pancakes, and Waffles

$\mathcal{H}$ONEY spread over toast, biscuits, or thickly buttered dark bread can provide the energy we need to start the day.

Honeys are fun to sample. For the gourmet who wishes to experiment, there is available at specialty shops a different honey for every day of the year. Native plants such as heartsease, raspberry, spearmint, borage, buck-wheat, star thistle, sage, and cotton give honey their own particular flavors and their names. There is tupelo honey from the swampy areas of Florida and Georgia; from Washington and Oregon, firewood honey, pale-gold and as thick as molasses; Texas contributes guajillo honey, water-white with a subtle milky shine; Hawaii furnishes alergoba honey; the banks of the Mississippi, river willow honey. There are all the lovely farm honeys that can be bought at roadstands, each one, like a French wine, having its *côte*. From abroad, the gourmet can buy Guatemalan coffee-tree honey, or Lolitza from Mexico. Scotland, Holland, and Norway export heather honey—each with a different texture, the Norwegian one particularly tough and sticky with lots of little air bubbles which make it a "sparkling" honey. There are wild thyme from Cyprus and Mt. Hymettus—the honey of the Olympian gods; Bavarian pine honey, thick and strong; rosemary honey from Narbonne in France, crystal-white and granular; acacia honey from Hungary, believed by many to be the finest in the world; lotus from India; eucalyptus from Australia; snow-white honeys from Siberia and black ones from Brazil; dogwood from Jamaica; black-locust from Italy;

and the rarest of all, wild flower honey gathered once a year in the Swiss Alps by the shepherds and treasured mostly for their own use.

Write to the American Honey Institute, Madison, Wisconsin, for the addresses of retail shops in your vicinity which carry some of these unusual honeys.

MY OWN CREAM OF WHEAT

½ cup liquid honey   3¾ cups milk
2 egg yolks   ½ cup cream of wheat
2 egg whites, beaten stiff   raisins (optional)

Bring milk to a rapid boil. Slowly sprinkle cream of wheat in it and stir until mixture thickens. Continue boiling with heat lowered for 5 minutes. Remove from fire. Allow to cool for a few seconds. Stir in egg yolks, ¼ cup honey, and raisins (if desired). Fold in egg whites. Place in a shallow casserole. Spread remaining honey on top by dribbling it from one side and tilting the casserole till it reaches the other side. Bake in hot oven (475°F) for 10 minutes.

CEREAL CROQUETTES

1 cup oatmeal, or cornmeal,   1 egg, beaten
    or cream of wheat   1½ cups bread crumbs
boiling water   butter
1½ tablespoons salt

Combine cornmeal, oatmeal, or cream of wheat with one cup cold water and the salt. Have 3 cups boiling water in top of double boiler. Stir in cereal mixture gradually. Cook and stir the mush over a quick flame for 10 minutes. Steam it covered over boiling water for 1 hour, or more. Stir frequently. When cold, roll cereal into balls or cut in squares. Dip in beaten egg, then in bread crumbs. Brown in butter slowly until golden brown.

    Serve with My Own Pancake Syrup or Waffle Sauce (below).
    Makes about 12 croquettes.

Note: Cooking time may be reduced by using quick-cooking cereals, and we suggest making this festive breakfast dish with cereal left over from the day before; there is something about getting up at the crack of dawn which would preclude our enjoyment of it.

MY OWN WAFFLE SAUCE

1 cup orange blossom honey   2 tablespoons butter
½ cup light cream   2 tablespoons Grand Marnier

Combine. Cook over a slow fire for 10 minutes. Pour into preheated pitcher and serve over waffles.

MY OWN PANCAKE SYRUP

Combine equal parts of honey, grenadine, or raspberry syrup. Slowly heat mixture and pour into warmed pitcher. May be made in quantity. Keeps indefinitely.

HOMINY PUDDING

⅔ cup hominy   1 tablespoon butter
3 cups milk   1 teaspoon grated lemon rind
2 eggs   ¾ cup honey

Boil hominy in milk 2 hours in double boiler. Beat eggs, honey, and lemon together. Pour hominy and egg mixture over second mixture. Add butter. Pour in buttered pudding dish. Bake in hot oven for 20 minutes.

CORN MIGUES

from Périgord in France

¾ cup cornmeal
1 tablespoon goose fat (or
   chicken fat)
¼ teaspoon salt

1 cup lukewarm water
2 eggs, beaten
½ cup bread crumbs

Mix all together in a bowl. This makes a very heavy dough. Divide into balls as big as an orange. Throw in salted boiling water. Simmer for ½ hour. Drain on a napkin.

Roll in beaten eggs and bread crumbs.

Pour honey over the Migues.

Note: A peasant's sweet. Good for a winter morning. In Périgord the Migues are often eaten just boiled, instead of bread.

OLD-FASHIONED ROLLED OATS AND HONEY ROLLS

½ cup rolled oats
½ tablespoon butter
¼ tablespoon salt
¾ cup boiling water

½ package dry yeast dis-
   solved in
1 tablespoon lukewarm water
¼ cup honey
2 cups sifted all-purpose flour

Combine oats, butter, salt with boiling water and cook, with occasional stirring, for 1 hour in a double boiler. Cool these ingredients until they are lukewarm. Add yeast and honey dissolved in lukewarm water. Add flour. Knead dough in bowl until the ingredients are well blended. Cover dough and allow it to rise in a warm place until doubled in bulk (for about 2 hours). Pinch pieces off with buttered hands and place them in greased muffin tins. Allow rolls to rise for about 2 hours. Bake them in a hot oven (425°F) for about 20 minutes.

Makes about 18 2-inch rolls.

Freeze in airtight container.

NORWEGIAN PANCAKES

4 eggs   1 cup flour
2 cups milk   ¼ teaspoon salt

Beat eggs at high speed. Lower speed and add rest of the ingredients. Beat until smooth. Mixture should be the consistency of thick cream.

Heat two or three heavy iron skillets (No. 8 is an excellent size). Butter them lightly. Pour ¼ cup batter into each, tilting the pans so that the batter covers the entire surface. When dry, turn quickly and brown other side. Fold pancakes in half, then into quarters to serve.

Makes about 12 pancakes.

Serve with lemon honey jelly (below).

LEMON HONEY JELLY

2½ cups honey   ½ cup liquid fruit pectin
¾ cup strained lemon juice

Blend honey and lemon juice in large saucepan. Bring to a full, rolling boil and add pectin, stirring constantly. Heat to a full boil. Boil 1 minute. When jelly flakes from mixing spoon, remove from heat. Skim and pour into hot sterilized glasses. Cover with paraffin.

Delicious with hot biscuits as well as meats.

Makes 5 glasses.

GINGERBREAD WAFFLES

1¼ cups cake flour
¾ teaspoon baking soda
½ teaspoon cinnamon
½ teaspoon ground ginger
¼ teaspoon ground cloves
¼ teaspoon salt

¼ cup melted butter
1 cup dark honey plus 2 ta-
    blespoons
1 whole egg, beaten
¾ cup strong black coffee

Sift flour twice with baking soda, spices, and salt. Combine butter, honey, and egg and beat 2 minutes with blender or 300 strokes. Add to dry mixture alternately with coffee. Bake. Serve hot with My Own Pancake Syrup or Waffle Sauce (see index).

Freeze in airtight containers. Do not defrost. Reheat in oven at 250°F.

A HONEY BRAN BREAD

1 cup honey
¼ cup bran
1 cup whole-wheat flour
1 teaspoon double-acting bak-
    ing powder
½ teaspoon salt

½ teaspoon baking soda
1 egg
¾ cup plus 2 tablespoons
    sour milk
½ cup honey
1 cup raisins

Combine bran, whole-wheat flour, baking powder, salt, and soda. Combine and beat egg, sour milk, and honey. Beat dry ingredients into liquid ingredients and add raisins. Place batter in 2 buttered 8 x 4 loaf pans. Allow to stand for 1 hour. Bake in moderate oven (375°F) for 1 hour or more.

Serve, very lightly toasted, with Swiss Honey (next page).

SWISS HONEY

½ cup butter   ½ cup heavy cream
¼ cup honey

Cream butter until soft. Add honey and beat until well
blended. Add cream gradually, beating with a rotary or electric beater until smooth and fluffy. Store in the refrigerator
until needed. Serve as a spread with waffles, pancakes, or
French toast.
   Makes 1 cup.

CARAWAY BRAN BREAD

1½ cups water   ¼ cup melted butter
1 cup scalded milk   2 tablespoons sugar
1 cup ready-to-eat whole bran   2 tablespoons salt
   cereal   1 teaspoon caraway seed
1 cake compressed yeast   5½ to 6 cups sifted flour
¼ cup honey

Combine water, milk, and whole bran cereal in large mixing
bowl. Cool to lukewarm. Add yeast, crumbled; mix well. Let
stand 5 minutes. Blend in honey, butter, sugar, salt, and caraway seed; mix well. Gradually add flour to form a stiff dough.
Knead on well-floured board until dough is smooth and satiny,
5 to 7 minutes. Place in buttered bowl and cover. Let rise in
warm place (85° to 90°F) until doubled in bulk, about 1½
hours. Punch down dough, turn, and cover. Let rise in warm
place for 30 minutes. Place dough on floured board and divide
in half; mold into two balls. Cover and let stand 15 minutes
for easy handling. Shape into loaves; place in well-greased

9 x 5 x 3-inch pans. Cover. Let rise in warm place until doubled in bulk, 45 to 60 minutes. Bake in moderate oven (375°F)
40 to 45 minutes.

Makes 2 loaves.

Freeze in foil. Warm for 20 minutes in wrapper at 250°F
without defrosting.

SWEET OATMEAL LOAVES

1½ cups milk
1 cup quick-cooking oatmeal
2 tablespoons salt butter
1¼ cups light cream
½ teaspoon salt

½ cup liquid clover honey
2 cakes yeast
2 cups unbleached flour
3 cups stone ground whole-
    wheat flour

Scald milk, add oatmeal, and cook 3 minutes. Add butter.
When melted, add cream, milk, honey, and salt. Cool. Add
yeast and beat well. Add whole-wheat flour to form a soft
dough. Knead until smooth. Let rise until double in bulk.
Shape into 3 loaves. Let them rise again until double in bulk
and bake at 375°F for 50 minutes.

Serve toasted or plain with your favorite honey.

Freeze in foil. Warm for 20 minutes in wrapper at 250°F
without defrosting.

MARTHA WASHINGTON'S HONEY OF ROSES

1 pint honey   1 pint red rose petals

Bring honey to a boil and remove any scum. Add rose leaves.
Set the pan in another pan of hot water and boil for half an
hour. More rose leaves may be added after 15 minutes, if avail-

able. Let stand for 10 minutes. Strain, while hot, into sterilized jars.

Note: Arab physicians in the fifteenth century considered this confection a valuable cure for tuberculosis. Dried rose petals from Ispahan were used.

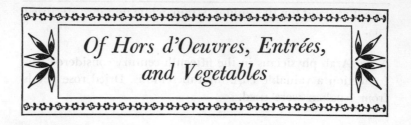

Of Hors d'Oeuvres, Entrées, and Vegetables

$\mathcal{E}$VEN though I searched through old chronicles, I have found only two instances of meats being flavored with honey during the Middle Ages. One of these is *Vyand Ryall,* an obvious distortion of the French words *Viande Royale* by the British envoy who reported on the wedding dinner of Jeanne de Navarre and Henry V: this dish consisted of rolled beef birds stuffed with ground rice and mulberries and properly salted and seasoned with wine, honey, and spices.

The second instance of honey used with meats was recorded by one of the master cooks of King Richard II of England— *Douce Âme,* a chicken stew with a poetic name:

"Take good cow milch and do it in a pot. Take parsley, sage, hyssop, savoury, and other good herbs and do in the milch seethe them. Take capons half roasted and smite them in pieces and do thereto pyn and honey clarified. Salt it and color it with saffron and serve it forth."

Oriental cookery, while it has many sweet-and-sour dishes prepared with refined sugar, boasts only a few that are flavored with honey, which was reserved for medicinal or ceremonial purposes. Symbolically, honey represents happiness, prosperity, and fertility. The most famous of honey-flavored Chinese wedding dishes is *Hsien Ching Ya Chioo,* boned ducks' feet and fresh ginger tips sauté.

It is in Poland, Germany, and Russia that most of the present-time sweet-and-sour dishes originated; the marinating

of meats in vinegar, honey, and spices was a substitute for refrigeration.

To this chapter, Yankee cookery has contributed original
and delicious ways of preparing vegetables. How these recipes
came into being is not known. The name of the adventurous
cook who first poured orange juice and honey over buttered
beets remains unfortunately unsung.

CHINESE JEE BOW GOI

[paper-wrapped chicken]

2 pounds raw chicken cut in 1½-inch squares, ¼ inch thick

Marinate chicken in:

4 tablespoons soy sauce
1½ tablespoons honey
½ jigger whisky

2 tablespoons plum jam
1 clove garlic, minced fine
1 teaspoon salt
½ teaspoon pepper

Drain chicken pieces. Wrap each individual piece in a small square of cooking parchment or foil. Fold it securely. Place in a roasting pan and bake for 1 hour at 350°F. When done, serve in paper wrapping. Dip with a toothpick in Red Bean Sauce (below).

RED BEAN SAUCE

1 No. 2 can red chili beans
1 tablespoon chili powder
1 teaspoon cinnamon
1 teaspoon cloves
¼ teaspoon black pepper

⅛ teaspoon anise
⅛ teaspoon fennel
⅓ cup water
1 clove garlic, minced
1 cup plum jam

Grind red chili beans through food mill and beat with egg beater. Mix well chili powder, cinnamon, cloves, black pepper, anise, and fennel. Add to ground chili beans. Mix well the water, garlic, and plum jam. Boil, stirring constantly, for 5 minutes. Add bean mixture and boil 10 minutes.

This sauce keeps well in refrigerator.

May be frozen. Warm in double boiler.

MOCK PEKING DUCK

[start 2 days ahead]

1 duck	1 teaspoon black pepper
1 cup honey	1 teaspoon anise
1 teaspoon cinnamon	1 teaspoon fennel
1 teaspoon cloves	

Stuff duck with paper towels and let stand uncovered on a rack in refrigerator for at least 2 days—change towels on second day. Remove towels from duck and let stand at room temperature (if possible, under an electric fan) for about 3 hours. Preheat oven to 450°F. Rub duck with honey, then rub inside and out with cinnamon, cloves, black pepper, anise, and fennel. Cook, breast down, on rack, in shallow pan, for 20 minutes, then turn over for about 40 minutes more. Carve bite-size pieces of meat. Can be reheated at 450°F for about 10 minutes.

This appetizer must be served Chinese style, in the center of a dish with toothpicks. Around it place 2-inch scallion strips and butter-flake or fan-tan rolls separated in sections. The pieces of duck are dipped individually, by each guest, in Red Bean Sauce (see preceding recipe) and then placed with a scallion strip in a sandwich made from two sections of the rolls.

PICKLED SALMON

[start 1 day ahead]

2 pounds salmon steak	1 tablespoon salt
½ cucumber	1½ tablespoons honey
2 onions, medium	2 cups water
3 bay leaves	1 tablespoon coarsely ground
parsley	pepper
2 cups tarragon vinegar	1 teaspoon dry mustard

Simmer salmon steak until tender in water salted to taste. Do not boil; boiling destroys the delicate texture of fish. Cool. Place cold salmon in a bowl. Cover with slices of cucumber and onion, bay leaves, and some parsley. Make a marinade of vinegar, salt, honey, water, pepper, and mustard. Pour it over the salmon and allow to stand for twelve hours before using.

Note: Halibut, sturgeon, or snapper may be treated in the same manner and served with green salad or as appetizers on crackers. It is better still when fried, as in this very old recipe from the *Compleat Court Book,* written by Patrick Lamb, master cook to Charles II, and published in London in 1726:

Dredge salmon with flour, fry it very brown in butter. Let your garnishings be only fried parsley. Serve it in plates, or little dishes, as hors d'œuvre.

SPICED EASTER EGGS CARDINAL

[start 2 days ahead]

6 medium-sized beets	½ teaspoon cloves
2 cups vinegar	½ teaspoon dry mustard
1 tablespoon honey	½ teaspoon dill
2 cloves garlic, sliced	1 teaspoon salt
½ teaspoon coriander seed	6 hard-boiled eggs

Leave one-inch stems on scrubbed beets. Boil until tender (18 minutes in pressure cooker). Cool. Peel and place them in solution of vinegar combined with all other ingredients listed. Allow to stand ½ hour. Discard beets. Place peeled hard-boiled eggs in marinade for 24 hours.

Serve with mayonnaise or use to decorate hors d'œuvres or salad.

PEANUT HONEYED GLAZED HAM

1 precooked ham
chunk-style peanut butter
   (the kind with chopped
   peanuts in it)

honey
ground cloves

Spread surface of ham with a mixture of peanut butter, honey, and cloves. (Use just enough strained honey to give the mixture a spreadable consistency and add ground cloves to taste.) Bake until crunchy crust forms on the ham.

Serve with Baked Beans and Glazed Onions (see index).

ORANGE HONEYED HAM

1 precooked ham
1 tablespoon grated orange
   peel

½ cup orange juice
1 cup honey
whole cloves

Bake ham, fat side up, uncovered, in slow oven (300°F) 25 to 30 minutes per pound. 45 minutes before ham is done remove rind and pour off most of fat in pan. Score in diagonal lines. Decorate with whole cloves. Blend grated peel, orange juice, and honey and spread mixture over ham. Return to oven. Baste frequently with mixture in pan. Remove from oven when ham is glazed and brown.

For decoration use pineapple slices and maraschino cherries in flower design. Hold in place on ham with whole cloves. Use angelica as stems and leaves. This is a basic recipe and any of the following glazes may be substituted.

HONEY GLAZES FOR COUNTRY HAMS

1 cup honey mixed with 1 cup apricot pulp

1 cup crushed pineapple with 1 cup honey

1 cup tart cherries and 1 cup honey

1 cup honey and ½ cup orange juice

1 cup honey and ½ cup cranberry sauce

1 cup honey and ½ cup cider

Serve with Gingered Carrots (see index).

MY OWN HAM STEAK

1 slice precooked ham (2 pounds)

1 teaspoon English mustard

½ cup American port wine

¼ cup honey

⅛ teaspoon allspice

pepper to taste

Spread mustard over ham, season with pepper and allspice. Pour honey and wine over it and bake in shallow casserole for 10 minutes. Broil just to get edges brown. Serve with garden-fresh peas and Sweet Potatoes Congolese (page 26).

GINGERED CARROTS

12 small carrots, cooked

3 cups honey

½ cup water

2 tablespoons powdered ginger

2 tablespoons butter

Cook above ingredients (except carrots) together until well thickened and pour over hot carrots.

BAKED BEANS

1 cup washed beans
2 cups cold water
¼ pound scored salt pork
¼ cup honey
½ teaspoon salt

½ teaspoon dry mustard
½ teaspoon ginger, if desired
½ teaspoon finely chopped
   onion

Soak beans in cold water overnight. In the morning drain off
any water that has not been absorbed. Cover beans with fresh
cold water and cook over low flame in a tightly covered saucepan. Do not allow the beans to boil. Let them simmer for 1¼
hours. Again drain the beans, saving the water. Prepare the
bean pot by placing salt pork in the bottom. Add beans, cover
with the following mixture: use bean water that has been
drained from beans and add to it honey; if no bean water was
left over, use plain boiling water. Mix salt, mustard, ginger,
and chopped onion with a little of the honey water. Add remainder of honey bean water to seasoning and pour over
beans. Place small pieces of salt pork on top. Cover bean pot
and bake in a slow oven about 6 hours. Uncover bean pot
during the last half hour of baking.

Serves 4.

Freeze in plastic container. Reheat in crock at 350°F, in
oven.

GLAZED ONIONS

16 small white onions
6 tablespoons butter

¼ cup honey

Cook onions in boiling salted water about 20 to 30 minutes,
or until tender. Drain. Let stand a few minutes to dry. Melt
6 tablespoons butter in pan. Add ¼ cup honey. When well

blended, add onions and cook slowly until browned and well glazed. Turn vegetables occasionally for an even glaze.

Serves 4.

SWEET POTATOES CONGOLESE

4 medium sweet potatoes   ¼ cup brandy
¼ cup honey   1 teaspoon grated lemon rind
Fritter Batter (see index).

Blanch sweet potatoes for five minutes in boiling water. Peel and slice them. Marinate them 1 hour in honey-brandy-lemon rind mixture without drying slices. Dip them in batter. Fry in deep fat until golden brown.

Serve piping hot.

Note: These fritters are excellent with roast turkey.

SWEET AND SOUR TONGUE

1 beef tongue   4 whole cloves
6 peppercorns   1 tablespoon vinegar
1 large onion, chopped   1 stick cinnamon
1 tablespoon butter   4 cloves
1 tablespoon flour   ¼ cup raisins
2 cups hot tongue liquid   ¼ cup brown sugar
½ teaspoon salt   1 tablespoon honey
1 tablespoon almonds, finely   juice of 1 lemon
   chopped

A 3-pound tongue serves 6 generously. Fresh, corned, or smoked tongues may be used. Corned or smoked tongues are improved by soaking in cold water for several hours before cooking.

Scrub tongue under running water. Place in deep kettle.

Add seasonings and boiling water to cover. Boil 10 minutes, then simmer for 3 to 5 hours, or until a fork will penetrate readily to the center. Let tongue remain in water until cool enough to handle. Peel off outer skin. Cut off back end, if there is one, and slice. Brown onion slightly in butter. Remove onion and set aside. Stir flour into hot butter and cook 3 minutes. Gradually add boiling liquid and salt and simmer gently until smooth and thickened, about 5 minutes. Add browned onions, almonds, cinnamon, cloves, and raisins. Mix well. Blend together brown sugar, honey, and lemon juice and stir into the mixture. Simmer about 10 minutes, stirring constantly. Correct seasoning to taste. Add sliced tongue and simmer until heated through. Serve hot with sauce.

May be prepared ahead.

Store in refrigerator in airtight container, or freeze.

Reheat in covered casserole in the oven, at 350°F.

BAKED SQUASH AND SAUSAGES

2 medium-size acorn squash   4 tablespoons honey
8 sausage links

Wash squash and cut in half lengthwise. Remove seeds. To each half add 1 tablespoon of honey and 2 pork sausage links. Bake at 400°F. until squash is tender and sausages brown.

Serves 4.

ESSIC FLEISCH

2 pounds brisket of beef   1 bay leaf
6 medium-size onions, sliced   boiling water
⅛ teaspoon salt   1 cup honey
dash each of pepper and   1 slice stale rye bread
    thyme   juice of 1 lemon

Place meat in large, heavy pan and add onions, salt, pepper, thyme, and bay leaf. Add boiling water and simmer until meat is tender, about 2½ hours. Add more boiling water as needed. When meat is almost done, add honey. Stir often while cooking and watch carefully so meat doesn't burn. Soak the bread in a little water, mash it, and when it's soft, add to meat. Stir well. Add 2 additional cups boiling water and lemon juice. Cook until meat browns well. Add salt and pepper, to taste.

Serves 6.

Serve hot or cold with a green salad.

Freezes very well in plastic or metal container. Reheat in slow oven in covered roasting pan.

CHINESE TIM-SHUN-YOK-KOW

[sweet and sour meat balls]

3 large green peppers	⅓ cup chicken bouillon
1 pound ground beef	1 small can pineapple
1 egg	chunks, drained
2 tablespoons flour	3 tablespoons cornstarch
½ teaspoon salt	2 teaspoons soy sauce
⅛ teaspoon pepper	½ cup vinegar
¾ cup oil or fat	½ cup honey
1 teaspoon salt	⅔ cup chicken bouillon

Cut peppers in 6 pieces each. Cook in boiling water until almost tender. Form ground beef into 16 small balls. Make a batter by beating together 1 egg, 2 tablespoons flour, ½ teaspoon salt, and dash of pepper. Dip meat balls into batter and place on a plate. Put oil or fat and salt in a preheated, heavy 10-inch frying pan. Place meat balls in pan and brown over moderate flame until golden brown on one side—about 5 minutes. Turn meat balls over and brown on other side. Remove meat balls to a hot platter and keep warm. Pour out all but 1 tablespoon of oil from pan. Add ⅓ cup chicken bouillon, pineapple, and green pepper. Cook over a very low flame for about 10 minutes. Blend together and add cornstarch, soy sauce, vinegar, honey, and ⅔ cup chicken bouillon. Stir constantly until juice thickens and the mixture is very hot—about 5 minutes. Pour over meat balls and serve immediately with hot, boiled rice.

Serves 4.

Freeze in plastic container. Reheat in oven in covered casserole at 350°F.

CHINESE TIM-SHUN-GAI-GONE

[sweet and pungent chicken livers]

3 large green peppers
2 tablespoons oil or fat
½ teaspoon salt
⅛ teaspoon pepper
¾ pound chicken livers
⅓ cup chicken bouillon

1 small can pineapple chunks, drained
3 tablespoons cornstarch
2 teaspoons soy sauce
½ cup vinegar
½ cup honey
⅔ cup chicken bouillon

Cut peppers in 6 pieces each and cook in boiling water until almost tender—about 8 minutes. Place oil, salt, pepper, and chicken livers in a preheated, heavy 10-inch frying pan and cook over a moderate flame, stirring constantly, until lightly browned. Remove chicken livers to a hot platter and keep warm. Put chicken bouillon, pineapple, and cooked green peppers in frying pan, cover tightly and cook over a very low flame for about 10 minutes. Blend together and add cornstarch, soy sauce, vinegar, honey, and chicken bouillon. Cook for a few more minutes, stirring constantly, until the juice thickens and the mixture is very hot—about 5 minutes. Pour over chicken livers and serve immediately with hot, boiled rice.

Serves 4.

CARROTS GLAZED IN HONEY

8 carrots   ⅓ cup strained honey
2 or 3 tablespoons butter

Boil whole small carrots until tender but still firm. Use a small enough amount of water so that it boils entirely away. Add butter and honey to cooked, dry carrots and simmer slowly until carrots are glazed and brown, turning once or twice.
    Serves 4.

HONEYED BEETS

1 can diced beets   ½ cup honey
2 tablespoons butter   ½ teaspoon salt
¼ cup orange juice   ½ teaspoon pepper
1 teaspoon grated orange peel

Put beets in casserole. Add butter, orange juice, orange peel, honey, and seasoning. Cook over moderate heat until liquid has evaporated and butter and honey form a glaze over the beets. Do not brown.
    Serves 4.

BAKED SLICED BEETS

20 small spring beets   1 tablespoon lemon juice
3 tablespoons butter   ⅛ teaspoon pepper
¼ cup honey   1 teaspoon salt
1 tablespoon finely chopped
    onion

Peel and slice the beets, chop them, and season them with the other ingredients. Butter a covered casserole. Place the beets in it and cover. Bake in a hot oven 400°F for 30 minutes. Stir twice and dust with chopped parsley before serving.

Serves 4.

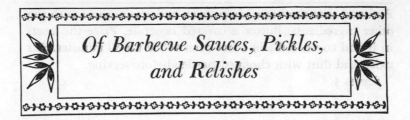

Of Barbecue Sauces, Pickles, and Relishes

$\mathscr{T}$HE Reverend Richard Warner, a very learned clergyman of the eighteenth century, wrote a treatise on the history of cooking from the time of Abraham. In it he assures us that the Romans basted their meats with a mixture of honey, asafetida, rue, and the distillation of the putrid essences of certain fish. Barbecue sauces seasoned with honey can be traced to these beginnings.

French and English mediæval cooks served roast meats smothered with *Sauce Cameline*—a mixture of wine, honey, vinegar, cinnamon, and hot peppers, cooked together, then thickened with bread. *Holy Water*, a sauce to be eaten with fowl, was made with rose water, honey, ginger, and marjoram.

The courtiers of King Richard the Lion-hearted were very fond of *Payn Fondew*, a relish made of fried bread, red wine, salt, raisins, honey, spices, and coriander seed. With fried meats they served *Payn Rangonn*, a praline type condiment of honey, bread crumbs, powdered ginger, and caramelized honey.

Around A.D. 1440 an anonymous French gourmet created a sauce made of bacon drippings, toast, stock, red wine, vinegar, cinnamon, mustard, pepper, and a very large proportion of honey. Because the contrast of sweet and hot elements in its composition brought to mind the countenance of a traitor, it was called *Sauce Trahison*. This sauce had a great vogue until the end of the Renaissance.

Most of the relishes in this chapter have come down to us

unchanged since the eighteenth century when they were used very abundantly in the winter to make up for the lack of vegetables. No formal Thanksgiving table was considered complete without seven sweet and seven sour relishes.

BARBECUE GLAZING SAUCE

3 cloves garlic
¼ cup olive oil
1 teaspoon salt
1 teaspoon freshly ground
  pepper
¼ teaspoon oregano

1 tablespon chopped fresh
  basil
1½ cups tomato purée
¼ cup strained honey
juice of 2 limes
½ cup red wine
¼ cup finely chopped parsley

Sauté finely chopped garlic in olive oil. Add salt, black pepper, oregano, basil, tomato purée, and honey. Simmer for 15 minutes and add lime juice and red wine. Blend well and simmer for another 10 minutes. Taste for seasoning. Just before removing from fire, add parsley.

Serve over roast meat.

Keeps 1 week in refrigerator. Freeze in plastic container. Reheat in double boiler.

HERBAL BARBECUE SAUCE

1 clove garlic, minced
1 small onion, minced
¾ teaspoon prepared mustard
1 tablespoon grated fresh
  horseradish
¼ tablespoon dried marjoram
¼ tablespoon dried thyme
¼ tablespoon dried savory
½ tablespon chopped parsley
1 teaspoon crushed red pepper

2 tablespoons tarragon vinegar
3 cups water
1 tablespoon Worcestershire
  sauce
⅔ cup butter
½ cup catsup
2 teaspoons honey
¾ teaspoon chili powder
¼ teaspoon coarsely ground
  pepper
¾ teaspoon salt

Combine all ingredients and simmer slowly for 40 minutes. Serve with hamburgers. Excellent, too, for dipping cocktail frankfurters.

Makes about 4 cups.

Keeps 1 week in refrigerator. Freeze in plastic container. Reheat in double boiler.

TOMATO BARBECUE SAUCE

½ pound bacon, diced
½ cup chopped celery
6 medium-sized fresh tomatoes quartered
2 tablespoons honey
½ cup chopped onion
1 tablespoon salt
1 tablespoon coarsely ground pepper
2 cups consommé

fresh herbs: tarragon, chervil, thyme, 1 sprig each; or ¼ teaspoon each dried herbs
⅛ teaspoon cayenne pepper
⅛ teaspoon powdered cloves
1 chopped green pepper
3 tablespoons chopped parsley

Brown bacon in skillet. Add onion and all seasonings. Simmer 5 minutes. Add tomatoes, then honey and consommé. Allow to simmer 40 minutes. Add chopped green pepper and parsley. Simmer another 5 minutes.

Serve with barbecued spareribs.

Keeps 1 week in refrigerator. Freeze in plastic container. Reheat in double boiler.

YELLOW TOMATO HONEY PRESERVE

[start 1 day ahead]

1 pound yellow tomatoes
½ cup honey
½ cup sugar
2 lemons

¼ tablespoon sliced preserved ginger
1 teaspoon mace
1 bay leaf

Wash tomatoes, dip them into boiling water for 1 minute, then into cold water, and slip off the skins. Put skinned tomatoes into an enameled preserving kettle with honey and sugar. Cover kettle with cheesecloth and allow to stand overnight in a cool place. Next morning pour liquid in kettle into a saucepan and boil it down until it is thick, skimming well. Add prepared tomatoes, lemons thinly sliced, but not pared, and sliced preserved ginger together with mace and bay leaf. Cook over a gentle flame until tomatoes are almost translucent. Pack at once into hot, sterilized pint jars and seal. Store in a cool place.

Makes 3 pints.

RUSSIAN HONEY BEET JAM

1 pound beets
honey

2 preserved ginger roots,
minced
almonds, sliced

Wash, peel, and cut beets into ½-inch slices, cook, and drain. Add one cup honey for each cup of beets and cook until thick. Flavor with ginger root and almonds.

Serve with cold meats.

HONEY MUSTARD FROM DIJON

[start 2 days ahead]

FIRST DAY

2 large onions, sliced
2 minced cloves of garlic

2 cups wine vinegar

SECOND DAY

2 teaspoons salt
¼ teaspoon cayenne pepper
1 cup dry mustard

½ cup strained first-day vinegar
1 tablespoon olive oil
2 tablespoons honey

Place together in a jar, or preferably an old cheese crock, first
three ingredients. Allow to stand 24 hours. Next day strain
vinegar. Reserve. Combine salt, cayenne pepper, mustard, and
½ cup of the strained vinegar. Bring remaining vinegar to a
boil and gradually add mustard mixture and simmer for 5
minutes. Cool. Add olive oil and honey.

Note: Keeps very well in small, tightly covered jars, and makes
a nice gift, too.

CHERRIES IN VINEGAR

5 pounds not-quite-ripe cherries
3 cloves
1 stick cinnamon
½ teaspoon grated nutmeg

1 teaspoon dried tarragon
  leaves
2 quarts vinegar
½ pound honey

Boil honey and vinegar 10 minutes. Cool. In the meantime,
put cherries in a bottle. Add cloves, cinnamon, nutmeg, and
tarragon. Pour honey-vinegar mixture into bottle. Cool. Steep
for 2 weeks.

Note: Wonderful with cold veal.

HONEY VINEGAR

½ cup honey
2 small cayenne peppers, half green, or ¼ teaspoon ground cayenne pepper

1 ground bay leaf
3½ cups wood-aged white wine vinegar

Put ingredients in quart bottle. Draw vinegar from cask into the bottle. Cork and leave 2 weeks on a sunny window sill. Strain before use.

Note: Best for barbecue sauces, sweet-and-sour dishes. Keeps indefinitely.

PICKLED SECKEL PEARS

14 pounds Seckel pears
1 teaspoon broken stick cinnamon

1 teaspoon whole cloves
1 quart cider vinegar
6 pounds honey

Pare pears. Tie spices in cheesecloth bag, add to vinegar and honey and heat to boiling. Add pears and cook until tender. Pears will look clear when tender. Remove them with spoon and fill sterilized jars. Remove spices. Boil syrup until thick, then pour over pears and seal.

Makes about 6 quarts.
Serve with cold fowl.

SPICED APPLE JELLY

7 pounds tart apples
juice of 1 lemon
2½ cups honey
4 cloves

1 stick cinnamon
1 bay leaf
2 berries allspice or ¼ teaspoon powdered allspice

Wash apples and quarter without peeling, leaving core and pits for additional pectin. To prevent them turning brown, gradually cover with cold water to which the juice of 1 lemon has been added. Bring to a boil in this liquid, then simmer over low heat until soft and tender. Drain through jelly bags, shifting pulp occasionally (without pressing) to keep jelly cloudless. Measure 4 cups of the juice into large kettle and boil 5 minutes. Add honey, also the spices tied in a small cheesecloth bag. Boil all together for about 8 minutes longer at a rolling speed, or until candy thermometer registers 220°F.

Repeat if there is more juice.

Makes four 8-ounce glasses.

BLUEBERRY PICKLE

4 quarts blueberries
5 cups honey
2 cups vinegar
1 teaspoon grated lemon rind

1 tablespoon whole allspice
2 sticks cinnamon
1 teaspoon whole cloves
⅛ teaspoon mace

Wash and drain berries. Make a light syrup by boiling sugar, vinegar with spices, tied in muslin bag, for 5 minutes. Add berries. Simmer until tender. Allow to stand overnight. Pack berries into hot, sterilized jars. Boil syrup 5 minutes. Pour over berries. Seal.

Makes 8 standard pickle jars.

Note: Excellent with cold roast game.

INDIA RELISH

12 large green tomatoes
1 red pepper
1 green pepper
4 large onions
1 tablespoon salt

1 cup dark honey
1 cup vinegar
1 tablespoon mustard seed
1 tablespoon celery seed

Chop tomatoes, onions, and peppers coarsely. Drain well. Add remaining ingredients and mix thoroughly. Cook slowly until vegetables are tender and mixture is thick, about 20 minutes. Turn into hot, sterilized jars, filling to ½ inch from top. Seal at once.

Makes 3 pints.

CORN RELISH

12 ears sweet corn	3 tablespoons mustard seed
8 green peppers	1 quart vinegar
4 red peppers	⅓ cup salt
4 green tomatoes	1 tablespoon turmeric
12 ripe tomatoes	1 cup sugar
1 quart onions	2 cups honey
5 tablespoons celery seed	1 cup dark corn syrup

Scrape corn from cobs. Cook until done. Chop remaining vegetables or put through food chopper. Add remaining ingredients. Cook until thick, 1 to 1½ hours. Turn into hot, sterilized jars filling to within ½ inch from top. Seal at once.

Makes 4 quarts.

MOUNT VERNON CHUTNEY

1 cup dried apricots, soaked 1 hour in water to cover	½ cup ginger root
	2 cloves garlic, minced
1 cup pitted dates	½ cup honey
4 cups sour red cherries, pitted	1 cup firmly packed brown sugar
1 cup seedless raisins	reserved apricot liquid
1 hot red pepper, seeded	1 cup wine vinegar
1 tablespoon salt	

Drain apricots and reserve liquid. Chop apricots, along with other fruit, hot pepper, and ginger root. Add garlic and salt and let mixture stand 1 hour. Add honey, brown sugar, apricot liquid, and vinegar. Bring mixture to a boil, lower the flame, and simmer 45 minutes or until chutney is very thick, stirring frequently.

Pack in jars.

Makes 3 pints.

CHAROSES

1 cup chopped apples
¼ cup chopped nuts
1 teaspoon kosher honey

½ teaspoon grated lemon rind
1 teaspoon cinnamon
2 tablespoons kosher wine

Mix all ingredients.

Note: This ceremonial complement to the Passover Feast, eaten on a piece of matzoth, symbolizes the mortar used by the Israelite slaves in the erection of the pyramids in ancient Egypt.

Matzoth is unleavened bread eaten during Passover. The custom of eating unleavened bread grew out of the Biblical narrative about the Exodus from Egypt. In their haste to depart, the Israelites carried with them dough which was still unleavened. As a yearly reminder, the people were commanded to eat this "bread of affliction." By extension the word *matzoth* is prefixed to noodles and meals which contain no leaven, and which are used in foods prepared during Passover week.

HONEY FRENCH DRESSING

⅔ cup olive oil
¼ cup tarragon vinegar or honey vinegar (see index)
¼ cup liquid honey

¼ teaspoon salt
⅛ teaspoon freshly ground black pepper
⅛ teaspoon dry mustard

Mix all ingredients together in a bowl. Pour over well-drained salad of Boston lettuce, avocado balls, and grapefruit sections. Sprinkle top with ground nuts. Try it on your favorite fruit combination salad, too.

Makes over 1 cup.

PINEAPPLE HONEY DRESSING

¼ cup lemon juice
½ cup honey

¼ teaspoon salt
3 tablespoons crushed pine-
apple

Mix lemon juice and honey. Add salt and crushed pineapple.

GOLDEN GATE SALAD DRESSING

2 eggs, slightly beaten
¼ cup honey
¼ cup lemon juice
½ cup orange juice

dash of salt
½ cup whipped cream, op-
tional

Combine ingredients and cook in double boiler until thickened, stirring frequently. Chill. If desired, fold in ½ cup cream just before serving. Serve with fruit salads.

Makes about 1 cup.

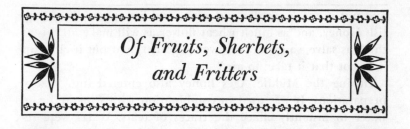

Of Fruits, Sherbets, and Fritters

A FIFTH-CENTURY book, *Joseph and Arsenath,* tells how an angel, eating a piece of honeycomb, put another into the mouth of Arsenath, and said: "Now thou hast eaten the bread of life and hast drunk the cup of immortality and received the unction of incorruption."

The ancients, in their time, thought of honey as a food having extraordinary medicinal properties. If we consider that they ate the comb with the valuable particles of "royal" jelly still clinging to it, we may find their claims justified when we acquire a more thorough knowledge of the properties of the miraculous queen-bee food.

Discorides claims that "the root of the lily beaten small with honey cleansed leprosy." Coriander "drunken with honey cureth the fever that cometh the third day after childbirth." The *Grete Herbal,* a seventh-century manuscript, says: "Honey is drunk against the biting of a Serpent or Mad dog and it is good for them that have eaten mushrooms or drunk poppy."

In a *Choice Manual on Rare and Select Secrets in Physics and Chirurgery* published in London in the early eighteenth century, the Right Honourable Countess of Kent gives a recipe for a "Green Salve for an Old Sore." "Take a handfull of groundsell, as much of houseleek, of marigold leaves a handfull, pick and wipe these Hearbs clean, but wash them not, then beat all these Hearbs in a wooden bowl, as small as possible then strain out all the juyce and put in a quantity of Hogs grease, as much as two Eggs, beat all these together again and put in ten Egg yolks and white and five spoonfuls of English Honey, and as much wheat flower as will make all this as thick as salve, so stir it very well together, and put it close up in a pot that it take no air."

During the Middle Ages honey also entered into beauty preparations. It was used in combination with wine and rose water to instantly efface the traces of tears. Warts were reported removed by an overnight application of a honey poultice and a yellow garden slug.

The *Toilet of Flora,* published anonymously in London in the eighteenth century, gives these recipes:

RECEIPT TO THICKEN THE HAIR: "Take roots of Maiden Vine, Roots of Hemp and cores of Soft Cabbages, of each 2 handfuls. Dry and burn them. Afterwards make a lye with the ashes. The head is to be washed with this lye three days success, the part having previously been well rubbed with honey."

A POMATUM FOR WRINKLES: "Take juice of white lily roots and fine honey, 2 oz. each, melted white wax 1 oz., incorporate the whole together. It should be applied every night and not be wiped off till morning."

FOR ROTTEN TEETH: "Make a balsom with a sufficient quantity of honey, two scruples of Myrrh in fine powder, a scruple of gum Juniper and 10 grams of rock alum. Frequently apply this to decayed tooth."

We have come to think of beauty and health as one. Our diets are scientifically charted, and the simple process of calorie-counting has made reducing comparatively painless.

As light desserts the many combinations of honey and fruit are excellent. Without going to the trouble of cooking, a teaspoon of a fine honey eaten with a raw fruit at the end of a meal is a healthy, low-calory way to satisfy the yearning for a sweet.

The modern gourmet, mindful of his health and waistline, will find in the following pages desserts and salads relatively low in calories and essential to good nutrition.

MY OWN PINEAPPLE ABLAZE

1 cup water
¾ cup honey
8 slices fresh pineapple
  (peeled and cored)
4 slices stale raisin bread or
  babka

2 tablespoons praline powder
  (see below)
¼ cup slivered or grated
  bleached almonds
½ cup kirsch

Make a syrup of honey and water. Boil, skim, and reduce to half the volume. Poach pineapple slices in this syrup for 6 minutes. Remove pineapple but keep syrup warm. In the meantime, remove crusts from four slices of bread or babka and brown them in butter. Arrange them in a square in the pan part of a chafing dish. Top with pineapple slices in a circle. Sprinkle with bleached almonds and praline powder. Light fire under chafing dish pan. Pour kirsch over the dessert. Set ablaze and eat with a little of the syrup passed around in sauceboat.

Note: Easy for a buffet supper because it can be prepared ahead of time—and spectacular, too.

PRALINE POWDER

¾ cup almonds (brown)   ¾ cup sugar

Put almonds and sugar in omelet pan over low flame. Stir until the sugar is a golden brown. Turn out on oiled platter. When cold, grind in meat grinder. Keep powder in preserve jar. Good over ice cream and in chocolate fudge sauce as well as in My Own Pineapple Ablaze.

MY OWN BANANAS ABLAZE

4 bananas	4 tablespoons honey
4 slices canned pineapple	½ cup bread crumbs
4 tablespoons melted butter	½ cup kirsch

Brush bananas with butter and honey. Roll them in bread crumbs. Bake 10 minutes in 450°F oven. Slip them through pineapple rings. Place in chafing-dish pan. Pour kirsch over fruit. Light flame under pan. When kirsch is warm light it.
Serves 4.

Note: A delicious chafing-dish quickie. Bananas may be baked ahead of time and reheated on chafing dish, thus keeping the oven clear for the hostess.

BARBECUED PINEAPPLE

1¼ cups honey	1 fresh pineapple, average size

Cut pineapple lengthwise in 8 sections. Place in a baking pan and drip honey over them. Allow to stand for ½ hour and then grill over slow (ash covered) coals.
Serve with frankfurters.

FRESH FRUIT CUP

2½ cups orange sections	1 cup orange juice
1 cup banana slices	dash of lemon juice
1 cup unpeeled, red-skinned apple slices	honey to taste
	berries or cherries for garnish

Combine and serve chilled as appetizer.
Serves 6.
For dessert, serve with Honey Snow Whip (below).

HONEY SNOW WHIP

2 egg whites   3 tablespoons honey
2 tablespoons lemon juice   dash of salt

Beat egg whites until frothy. Add lemon juice and salt. Continue beating until whites are stiff. Trickle honey over egg whites a little at a time and beat thoroughly after each addition. If egg whites and honey separate on standing, beat with rotary egg beater and dressing will resume former consistency. Serve with a combination of fresh fruits, bread or steamed pudding.

STUFFED MELON

A ripe Persian melon   1 cup wild strawberries
½ cup orange honey   ¼ cup Grand Marnier

Cut off top of melon. Empty seeds and liquid. Cut out melon balls with a small scoop. Reserve. Pour honey in melon and dribble all around to glaze the inside. Fill with strawberries and melon balls. Add Grand Marnier. Cover with top slice. Seal opening with butter and leave melon in refrigerator 2 hours before serving.

BROILED HONEYED GRAPEFRUIT

For each grapefruit half:

2 teaspoons honey   ⅛ teaspoon mace (optional)
⅛ teaspoon cinnamon   ½ teaspoon butter

Remove seeds from halves of grapefruit. Core and loosen sections. Spread with honey and sprinkle with cinnamon and mace. Dot with butter. Brown under moderate flame of broiler unit. Serve at once.

HONEYED FIGS

1 cup honey
5 tablespoons wine (port for
    black figs, angelica or
    muscatel for white figs)

12 ripe figs (black or white),
    peeled
juice of 2 small lemons
few drops of vanilla, if
    desired

Boil honey and wine together gently to make a medium-thick syrup. Add peeled figs and cook to a very thick syrup, then add lemon juice and vanilla and cook a few minutes longer, or until again very thick. Pour hot into sterilized jars or glasses; cover with lids. It is not necessary to seal them tightly.

Yield: two 6-ounce jars.

To make Glacé Figs, cook as directed above until the syrup is very, very thick and has almost disappeared, then remove from the heat, spread the figs on platters, and dry in the sun, turning occasionally, until they are firm but not hard. Store in thin layers in tin boxes lined with heavy waxed or parchment paper.

HONEYED AMBROSIA

6 oranges
honey

½ cup grated coconut

Peel and slice oranges. Arrange half the slices in a serving dish and sprinkle with half the coconut. Trickle honey over coco-

nut and fruit. Cover with remaining slices, sweeten with more
honey, and top with remaining coconut.
  Serves 6.

Note: If dried coconut is used, soak in milk awhile. Drain. It
will have a fresher flavor.

FRENCH FRUIT MÉLANGE

[have on hand a bottle of good brandy]

1 quart strawberries	¼ tablespoon allspice
1 cup honey	1 cinnamon stick
¼ tablespoon thyme	1 tablespoon grated lemon
¼ tablespoon cloves,	and orange rind
powdered	

Use a wide-mouthed earthen crock—the kind found in an-
tique shops. Be sure it has a cover. Hull strawberries and
dump them in crock with all ingredients and enough brandy
to keep berries covered. Put cover on crock and use freezer
tape or adhesive tape to seal it on the jar. Allow this to stand
for a week. As the season progresses repeat process with
stemmed cherries, raspberries, red currants, gooseberries,
peaches, blackberries, different kinds of plums, elderberries,
adding fruit until the crock is full. Seal with fresh tape after
each addition. The crock should be full. Allow to remain
sealed until Christmas. Serve with puddings, ice creams, etc.
and use liquid as a base for punches.

Note: A very large glass candy, or apothecary, jar will do as
well as a crock if lid is sealed on with tape.

FROZEN FRUIT AND BERRY PURÉE

strawberries
cherries
raspberries
apricots
currants
blackberries
or mulberries may be used for this recipe

Wash and trim fruit, heat it without boiling to preserve color
and flavor, and force it through a fine sieve. Mix purée with a
small amount of honey, to taste, and package for freezing immediately in pint plastic containers.

Use later for fruit cream sherbets, fruit purée creams, and
fruit sauces.

Note: Special purée strainers of the "food mill" type may be
purchased in fine hardware stores. They are a great help. A
baby-food strainer may be used, too.

FRUIT PURÉE CREAM

1 envelope gelatin	1 cup honey
2 tablespoons cold water	2 cups heavy cream, whipped
2 cups fruit purée, fresh or frozen	brandy

Soften gelatin in cold water. Dissolve over hot water. Combine
dissolved gelatin with fruit purée, honey, and whipped cream.
Flavor with brandy. Pour cream into a mold and chill. Unmold and serve.

Makes 6 portions.

JEANNE OWEN'S STRAWBERRY AND
HONEY CREAM

1 cup heavy cream with a   2 tablespoons strawberry
   pinch of salt   juice
½ cup honey

Whip cream and gradually pour in honey and juice. Serve in
a large glass bowl with a bowlful of fresh picked strawberries.

JEANNE OWEN'S HONEY PEARS

4 pears   3 tablespoons domestic
¼ cup granulated sugar   brandy or kirsch
¼ cup water   fresh raspberries
½ cup honey

Core and peel pears leaving them whole. Put sugar and water
in saucepan over low flame. When sugar has melted add
honey. Poach pears in syrup until tender but not mushy. Cool
in syrup. When syrup is cool add brandy or kirsch. Serve pears
on individual dishes and surround them with fresh raspberries. Pour some of the syrup over all the fruit.

HONEYED KUMQUATS

2 cups kumquats   2 cups honey
whole cloves   1½ cups water

Wash kumquats and cover with boiling water. Steep 5 minutes. Drain. Stick 1 whole clove in each fruit. Boil honey and
water together and reduce to ⅔ volume. Skim. Poach fruit in
syrup for 20 minutes. Store in tightly covered jars.

CANDIED BANANAS

6 medium-sized, not quite   2 tablespoons butter,
    ripe bananas   creamed, with
¼ cup Chablis   1 tablespoon finely ground
½ cup honey, light   almonds

Place peeled bananas in shallow buttered dish. Pour honey
and wine over them. Dot with butter. Bake 15 minutes in hot
oven 450°F, basting 3 times.

FRUIT SANDWICH SPREAD

¼ cup chopped prunes   ¼ cup chopped figs
¼ cup raisins   ¼ cup honey
¼ cup chopped dates   2 tablespoons lemon juice

Chop fruits all together, add honey and lemon juice and blend
well. Keeps well in refrigerator jar. Serve with whole-wheat
or brown bread.

BLENDED FRUITS

APPLE

2 tablespoons unsweetened   ½ cup unpeeled diced eat-
    apple juice   ing apples
2 tablespoons honey

Put ingredients in electric blender and place cover on. Run
blender from 10 seconds to 2 minutes.
    Serves 3.

BLENDED FRUITS

PLUM

2 tablespoons water   2 tablespoons honey
½ cup pitted plums

Put ingredients in electric blender and place cover on. Run
blender from 10 seconds to 2 minutes.
   Serves 3.

APRICOT NECTAR

½ cup orange juice   2 teaspoons honey
¼ cup soaked dried apricots

Put ingredients in electric blender and place cover on. Run
blender from 20 seconds to 1 minute.
   Makes ¾ cup.

SWEET POTATO DESSERT, MEXICAN STYLE

4 medium-sized sweet   2 cups grape juice
   potatoes   1 teaspoon cinnamon
1½ cups honey

Peel and cut potatoes in halves, lengthwise. Place in Pyrex
baking dish. Warm grape juice and mix with honey and cinnamon. Pour over potatoes and bake at 400°F until tender and
candied. Cool a little. Serve warm with whipped cream.

MEXICAN MANGO SHERBET

6 cups milk
1 pint canned mangoes
2 cups honey

2 tablespoons gelatin, dissolved in ½ cup cold water

Scald milk and mix with honey and gelatin. Place in freezer tray. When liquid begins to freeze, stir and add mashed mangoes. Return to freezer tray. Serves 8.

Note: I put my mangoes in blender for 1 second.

GUAVA SHERBET

6 cups milk
1 pint canned guavas
1 tablespoon gelatin dissolved in

½ cup water
2 cups honey
1 cup minced walnuts

Scald milk and mix with honey and gelatin. Place in freezer tray. When liquid begins to freeze, stir and add mashed guavas. Return to freezer tray. Serves 8.

HONEY AND BANANA SHERBET

juice and grated rind of 1 lemon
juice of 2 oranges
3 bananas

½ cup honey
3 cups water
2 egg whites, stiffly beaten

Mash bananas to a pulp. Add lemon and orange juice and rind. Bring water to a boil. Dissolve honey in it. Add to fruit and mix well. Cool and fold in egg whites. Pour into refrigerator tray to freeze, stirring twice as it begins to set. Serves 4.

A PINEAPPLE SHERBET

1 large pineapple   ½ cup honey
juice of 2 lemons

Pare pineapple and grate fine. Cook for about 10 minutes in
½ cup honey and 1 quart of water. Strain and let cool. Freeze
about 6 minutes in ice cream freezer, or in freezer tray, until
it begins to set. Repeat twice and serve mushy with crushed
fresh pineapple or whipped cream.
    Serves 6.

FRUIT CREAM SHERBET

4 egg whites   2 tablespoons lemon juice
⅛ teaspoon salt   2 cups fruit puréc
½ cup honey   2 cups cream, whipped
½ cup sugar

Beat egg whites with salt until they are stiff. Gradually beat in
sugar and honey and continue to beat until the meringue is
thick and glossy. Stir in lemon juice and fruit purée from
frozen fruit. Fold in whipped cream. Pour the mixture into a
freezing tray and freeze until mushy. Transfer to a chilled
bowl and beat vigorously until smooth. Return to tray and
continue to freeze at coldest temperature control until sherbet
is solid. Serves 8.

HONEY PEPPERMINT SHERBET

1½ teaspoons gelatin   ⅓ cup honey
2 tablespoons water   ¾ cup crushed peppermint
½ cup milk   stick candy
2½ cups cream

Soak gelatin in cold water. Heat milk and cream and add
honey; mix well. Add gelatin slowly, stirring constantly to prevent lumping. (Thoroughly chill if you wish to shorten freezing time.) Pour in freezing trays with crushed candy and freeze
until mushy. Stir. Repeat twice. If bits of the candy are desired
in the sherbet, add it after the mix has become semi-solid. Unsweetened chocolate (1 square), cut into very small pieces, may
be added. Serves 4.

Serve with Chocolate Almond Sauce (below).

CHOCOLATE ALMOND SAUCE

4 squares bitter chocolate	⅓ cup honey, liquid
1 tablespoon Cointreau	⅓ cup shredded toasted al-
⅛ teaspoon salt	monds

In double boiler, melt chocolate with Cointreau and stir until smooth. Add salt and honey. Continue cooking over hot
water until mixture is thoroughly blended. Then stir in almonds. Cover. Remove from fire and allow sauce to steam for
15 minutes, stirring occasionally.

Serve lukewarm.

MY OWN LOCUST OR ELDERBERRY
FLOWER FRITTERS

12 clusters of flowers (locust	¼ cup honey
or elderberry)	1 recipe batter (see below)
¼ cup cognac	

Marinate clusters of flowers ½ hour in cognac and honey mixture. Dip flower clusters in batter and fry in deep vegetable

shortening until golden brown. Arrange on folded napkin. Dust with confectioner's sugar.

Serves 4.

BATTER FOR FRUIT OR FLOWER FRITTERS

½ pound flour
½ teaspoon salt
¼ cup melted butter

1 can beer, more if needed
2 egg whites, whisked to a froth

Put flour, salt, and melted butter in a bowl and dilute gradually with beer and a little lukewarm water. When about to use the batter, mix in the egg whites.

Note: Keep this batter thin, do not stir too much.

ALSATIAN SCHAUKELE

(*a fritter*)

1 egg
1 cup crystallized honey

¾ cup coarsely ground almonds
4 cups flour (more or less)

Beat eggs and honey in blender full speed for 10 minutes. Gradually add almonds and flour. Beat 5 minutes more. This dough should be rather stiff. Add more flour if necessary. On a floured board roll into the shape of cigars. Fry in deep fat until golden brown. Dust with confectioner's sugar.

Serves 4.

MOROCCAN LEBAS-EL-AAROUSSA

2 cups sifted all-purpose flour
1 egg

1 cup granulated sugar
⅛ teaspoon salt
2 tablespoons water

Mix all ingredients together until smooth. Roll out to ¼-inch thickness. With a sharp knife cut to finger lengths. On a floured board finish giving strips a finger shape by rolling lightly. Fry till golden in deep fat. Roll in honey. Serve hot.

Serves 4.

Note: The title, in Arabic, means "the bride's finger."

MOROCCAN MESELMEN

2 cups stone ground whole-
    wheat flour
⅛ teaspoon salt
½ cup sugar
2 tablespoons olive oil

2 tablespoons water
1 cup lukewarm honey for
    use as a syrup
¼ cup ground nuts

Work ingredients together lightly. Roll to ¼-inch thickness on floured board. Cut out in star or round shapes. Throw in deep fat and brown. Sprinkle with ground nuts and honey.

Makes 12 cakes.

Note: The Arabs use the nuts from the native pine cones, blanched and slivered. These nuts can be found in Italian and Armenian markets.

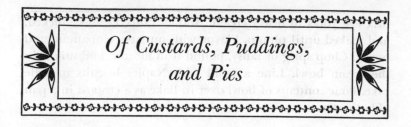

Of Custards, Puddings, and Pies

*M*ANY desserts in this section contain a combination of milk, dried fruit, honey, and nuts. These ingredients are ideal to supplement the meals of convalescents, growing children, and people wishing to gain weight.

Most of us have learned, in the interest of our health, to count calories. It is possible even on the strictest of reducing diets to enjoy an occasional custard, pudding, or any rich food, provided we forego other sources of calories so that the sum total of our daily calorie intake remains unchanged.

In general, puddings, custards, and pies require few last-minute exertions and are simple to make in advance. I chose to include a few desserts more difficult to make because I felt the results will justify your added efforts.

You will find a wide choice of flaming puddings; I feel they deserve a greater place on our table. They add a gay touch to a winter meal and are easy to prepare. Steamed a day ahead, and stored overnight in the mold or bowl in which they were steamed, they may be reheated easily.

MRS. LESLIE'S EIGHTEENTH-CENTURY TANSY

6 egg yolks
2 cups heavy cream
¼ cup currants
nutmeg

cinnamon
honey
1 large sprig tansy
Naples biscuits or stale cake

Mix egg yolks in heavy cream. Add currants, cleaned, picked, and soaked until plump. Flavor with nutmeg, cinnamon, and honey. Chop sprig of tansy, pound it in mortar, and mix it in the cream bowl. Line a mold with Naples biscuits or stale cake. Pour contents of bowl over it. Bake as a custard in a pan of hot water.

Note: Naples biscuits is another name for ladyfingers.

MOUSSE AU MIEL

[honey mousse]

1 pint heavy cream	**1½ cups strained honey**
6 egg yolks	**3 egg whites beaten stiff**

Beat egg yolks together with the honey until thoroughly blended and light. Whip 1 pint heavy cream, blend it with the mixture, and fold in the egg whites. Pack in a mold and freeze without stirring again.

Note: A buckwheat or orange or rose honey would be particularly suitable for this dessert.

APPLE CUSTARD

¾ cup hot milk	**⅓ cup raw, diced, unpeeled**
1 egg	**apples**
1 tablespoon honey	

Place all ingredients, except egg, in electric blender. Put cover on. Run until contents are thoroughly blended—about 1 minute. Remove cover and add egg. Blend 3 seconds. Pour into 3 buttered 4-ounce custard cups. Place cups in pan of hot water.

Bake in a moderate oven (325°F) about 20 minutes. Or place on a rack in a saucepan with water 1 inch above rack. Cover tightly and cook for 15 or 20 minutes over very low heat, keeping water below boiling point.

Serves 3.

All custards will keep 24 hours in refrigerator. For perfect flavor cover with foil.

PEACH CUSTARD

¾ cup hot milk   ⅓ cup drained canned
1 egg   peaches
1 tablespoon honey

See directions for Apple Custard (above), substituting peaches for apples.

STRAWBERRY CUSTARD

¾ cup hot milk   1 tablespoon honey
1 egg   ½ cup strawberries

See preceding directions for Apple Custard, substituting strawberries for apples.

BING CHERRY CUSTARD

¾ cup hot milk   ⅓ cup pitted raw Bing
1 egg   cherries
1 tablespoon honey

See preceding directions for Apple Custard, substituting Bing cherries for apples.

PUMPKIN CUSTARD

¾ cup hot milk   1 tablespoon honey
1 egg   ⅓ cup cooked pumpkin

Season to taste with allspice, nutmeg, cloves, and cinnamon.
Then proceed according to directions for Apple Custard (page
61), substituting pumpkin for apple.

COTTAGE CHEESE CUSTARD

¾ cup hot milk   1 tablespoon honey
1 egg   ⅓ cup cottage cheese

See directions for Apple Custard (page 61), substituting cottage cheese for apples.

RAISIN CUSTARD

¾ cup hot milk   ⅓ cup soaked until plump
1 egg   dried brown raisins
1 tablespoon honey

See directions for Apple Custard (page 61), substituting raisins
for apples.

APRICOT CUSTARD

¾ cup hot milk   ⅓ cup soaked until plump
1 egg   dried apricots
1 tablespoon honey

See directions for Apple Custard (page 61), substituting apricots for apples.

PRUNE CUSTARD

¾ cup hot milk
1 egg
1 tablespoon honey

⅓ cup soaked until plump
pitted dried prunes

See directions for Apple Custard (page 61), substituting prunes for apples.

AN ORANGE PUDDING

the peel of 6 oranges, grated
1 package ladyfingers
yolks of 6 eggs beaten with 4
    whites

⅛ teaspoon nutmeg
¼ cup honey
⅛ teaspoon salt

Boil ladyfingers in cream and run through sieve. Add eggs and orange peel. Bake in pan half filled with hot water for one hour at 300°F.

Store in refrigerator in airtight container. Will keep 24 hours.

MY OWN TURINOIS

[start 1 day ahead]

1 large can chestnuts (about
    3 cups cooked and
    skinned)
½ cup sweet butter, liquid

½ cup grated semi-sweet
    chocolate
½ cup orange honey
whipped cream, about ½ cup

Drain chestnuts and place them in electric blender, reserving liquid. Dissolve gelatin in liquid. Add all other ingredients to chestnuts. Blend. Pour into loaf pan and chill in refrigerator overnight. Unmold and cut into slices ½ inch thick. Garnish each slice with 1 teaspoon of whipped cream in center.

Serves 6.

GREEK RIZOGOLO

2 cups milk	¾ cup washed rice
½ cup water	2 egg yolks, beaten
4 tablespoons honey	powdered cinnamon, nutmeg

Add water to milk and bring to a boil. Stir in rice. Cook until very tender. Season with nutmeg. Pour in honey, stir and cook 2 minutes more. Remove from heat and stir in yolks. Pour into serving dish and sprinkle top with powdered cinnamon.

Serve very cold.

Store in airtight container in refrigerator. Will keep 24 hours.

PERSIAN PEACH DELIGHT

[start 2 days ahead]

4 cups top milk	with 2 tablespoons kirsch
½ cup rose water	2 cups whipped cream
4 tablespoons honey	1 small can crushed pineap-
2 cups rice	ple, drained and mari-
3 egg yolks, beaten	nated in
2 envelopes gelatin	¼ cup kirsch
2 tablespoons grated orange	2 tablespoons slivered (on
rind	the grater) blanched al-
2 cups My Own Pancake	monds
Syrup (see index) mixed	6 fresh peach halves

Put top milk in double boiler. When it boils, stir in rice. Cook 1½ hours. Reserve. Blanch peach halves in boiling water, peel, and cook until soft in a syrup made of sugar and water in equal parts, flavored with 1-inch vanilla bean. Drain and reserve. Meanwhile, soak gelatin in rose water. Reserve. When done, mix half of the rice mixture with egg yolks and orange rind. Turn out on platter. Cool. Rub other half through strainer. Dissolve soaked gelatin with ¼ cup boiling water. Mix with strained rice. Add marinated pineapple. Fold in whipped cream. Put almonds in bottom of rinsed and wet ring mold. Store ring and rice pudding in refrigerator overnight. Shortly before serving, make walnut-size balls with reserved rice pudding. Fry till golden-brown in deep fat. Drain. Turn out rice ring. Place peach halves on ring. In the middle put the very hot rice croquettes. Pour heated sauce over dish and serve.

Note: Superb and worth *all* the trouble.

HONEY SOUFFLÉ

4 eggs, separated	½ teaspoon nutmeg
1 tablespoon kirsch	½ cup clarified butter
1 cup granulated sugar	1 cup strained honey
1 tablespoon pastry flour	1 teaspoon ground pistachio
¼ teaspoon salt	nuts

Beat egg yolks and kirsch until thick and lemon-colored. Gradually add sugar sifted with pastry flour, salt, and nutmeg, beating all until very light. Beat together butter and strained honey and add to mixture a little at a time, still beating briskly after each addition. Fold in stiffly beaten egg whites. Turn into a large buttered soufflé dish, filling only ⅔ of it to allow room for rising. Sprinkle with ground pistachio nuts and set dish in pan of hot (not boiling) water. Bake 35 to 40 minutes in a moderate oven (375°F).

Serve at once with Raspberry Sauce (over).

Serves 6.

RASPBERRY SAUCE

1 pint fresh raspberries   ¼ cup water
¼ cup honey   1½-inch vanilla bean

Pick over raspberries. Wash by placing in a colander and letting cold water run gently over them, shaking the colander frequently. Drain, then crush. Add honey, vanilla bean, and water and mix well. Bring to the boiling point; simmer gently for 5 minutes; press through a fine sieve.

May be made in quantity. Store in airtight container. Will keep indefinitely in refrigerator.

Note: Appropriate for any hot or cold pudding, as well as frozen desserts and Peach Melba.

ROMANIAN CATAÏF

1 quart milk   2 tablespoons vanilla extract
1 pound vermicelli   4 eggs, beaten
1 cup raisins   1 cup heavy cream
1 inch vanilla bean or   2 tablespoons honey—twice

Cook vermicelli rapidly in milk in a deep pot 10 minutes. Drain carefully. Pour vermicelli, mixed with raisins, into well-buttered pudding mold. Beat eggs and cream and honey lightly. Pour over vermicelli and bake in hot oven (400°F) for 20 minutes.

Serve hot or cold. Wonderful with My Own Pancake Syrup or Raspberry Sauce (see index).

Store in airtight container. Will keep 24 hours in refrigerator.

OLD ENGLISH PLUM PUDDING

½ cup finely crumbled suet   4 eggs
2 cups raisins, packed   1 teaspoon double-acting
1 cup currants, packed   baking powder
½ cup brown sugar, packed   ½ teaspoon salt
½ cup citron   ½ teaspoon allspice
2 cups flour   ½ teaspoon nutmeg
½ cup milk   ½ teaspoon cinnamon
½ cup honey   ¼ teaspoon pepper
1 cup walnuts, chopped

Dredge fruit and nuts with flour. Pour into well floured cloth. Tie, allowing room for expansion. Cook three hours in boiling water.

Serve with Sugarless Honey Hard Sauce (see index).

Makes 1 large pudding.

Store overnight in mold or bowl. Reheat by steaming 10 minutes or until thoroughly warm.

Freeze in airtight container. When re-serving, steam until thoroughly warm.

SUET PUDDING

1 cup suet, chopped fine   1 teaspoon salt
1 cup honey   1 teaspoon baking soda
1 cup bread crumbs   1 cup raisins, seeded cur-
½ cup sour milk   rants, or any preserved
1½ cups flour   fruit
1 teaspoon cinnamon

Add baking soda to milk. Mix well with the other ingredients. Turn into well-buttered pudding mold, cups, or coffee cans.

Cover closely with buttered paper or fitted covers. Tie down
covers. Put into kettle of boiling water on a rack or trivet
with water 1 inch from covers of the cups. Cover kettle and
steam 3 hours if in a mold, or 1 hour if in cups. Turn out of
molds and serve on hot dish with Whipped Honey Sauce (below).

WHIPPED HONEY SAUCE

3 egg whites   ½ teaspoon grated lemon or
½ teaspoon salt   orange rind
½ cup honey

Beat egg whites with salt until stiff. Beat honey in very slowly
and continue beating until mixture thickens. Add grated
lemon or orange rind.

Serve at once over cake or ice cream.

WHOLE-WHEAT PUDDING

2 cups whole-wheat flour   ½ cup honey
½ teaspoon baking soda   1 cup stoned and chopped
½ teaspoon salt   raisins or dates or
1 cup milk   1 cup ripe berries

Mix ingredients in order given. Steam 2½ hours and serve
with whipped cream.

Store overnight in the mold or bowl. Reheat by steaming 10
minutes or until thoroughly warm. Freeze in airtight container. When re-serving, steam until thoroughly warm.

Note: One cup of figs, stewed prunes, or chopped apples makes a pleasing variety.

OATMEAL DATE PUDDING

½ pound dates, chopped   ⅔ cup water
1 cup rolled oats   ½ teaspoon baking soda
2 eggs   ¼ teaspoon salt
½ cup honey   juice of ½ lemon

Mix all ingredients and steam in buttered mold 3 hours.
Serve with Honey Cream Sauce I (below).

HONEY CREAM SAUCE I

⅓ cup whipping cream   1 teaspoon lemon juice
¼ to ½ cup honey

Whip cream until thick, add honey and lemon juice, whipping constantly.

SUGARLESS HONEY HARD SAUCE

⅓ cup butter   grated rind or rum, brandy,
¾ cup honey   sherry, etc.
juice of 1 orange

Beat butter until soft, adding honey gradually. Season with orange rind and juice; or with rum, brandy, sherry, etc.
Make in quantity. Freeze in small packages.
Serve frozen over hot desserts.

INDIAN TAPIOCA PUDDING

3 tablespoons corn meal   ⅛ teaspoon cinnamon
3 tablespoons minute tapioca   ⅛ teaspoon ginger
2 tablespoons sugar   3 cups hot milk
¼ teaspoon salt   ½ cup honey

Mix together corn meal, tapioca, sugar, salt, cinnamon, and
ginger. Pour hot milk and honey over this. Pour into buttered
baking dish and bake in moderately hot oven (325°F), stirring
frequently.
Serve with warm Honey Cinnamon Sauce (below).

HONEY CINNAMON SAUCE

1 cup honey   ½ teaspoon cinnamon
¼ cup butter   ⅛ teaspoon salt

Heat honey in top of double boiler, stir in butter and cinnamon, mixed with salt. Mix well.
Serves 6.

STEAMED CHRISTMAS FRUIT SPONGE

¼ cup honey   6 dried figs, pitted and
¼ teaspoon baking soda   chopped
3 eggs, well beaten   10 dates, pitted and chopped
½ cup cake flour   8 prunes, pitted and chopped
½ cup stone ground whole-   ½ cup mixed candied fruits
   wheat flour   ½ cup sherry
1 teaspoon baking powder   2 lumps of sugar
⅓ teaspoon salt   1 cup good brandy
4 tablespoons finely ground   Honey Almond Sauce
   nuts

Cream honey and eggs until white and foamy. In another bowl sift together flour, whole-wheat flour, baking soda, baking powder, and salt. Mix in nuts and fruit. Then add sherry to egg-honey mixture and blend this thoroughly with flour-fruit mixture. Turn batter into buttered melon or pudding mold. Adjust lid tightly and steam for 2¾ hours. Place lumps of sugar in heated ladle with brandy. Set it ablaze. Ladle over the sponge pudding. Serve hot with Honey Almond Sauce (see index).

CLAN DOUGLAS PLUM AND CARROT PUDDING
[start 2 days before Christmas]

FIRST DAY

2 cups currants, soaked in hot water until plump

1 cup pitted, chopped prunes

½ cup candied citron

2 large, tart apples, cored and chopped with 1 tablespoon lemon juice

½ cup hard cider or Calvados liqueur

1 teaspoon grated lemon rind

2 grated medium carrots

1 cup grated blanched almonds

1½ cups bread or brioche crumbs

½ cup brandy

¼ cup black rum

SECOND DAY

1 cup beef suet, ground finely

¼ cup sweet butter

1 teaspoon salt

1 cup flour, sifted with

1 teaspoon cinnamon

½ teaspoon allspice

½ teaspoon powdered cloves

¼ teaspoon nutmeg

¼ teaspoon mace

¼ teaspoon black pepper

½ cup sugar

½ cup honey

Combine in a mixing bowl currants, citron, apples, lemon juice, hard cider, grated lemon rind, carrots, and almonds, bread crumbs, brandy, and rum. Soak overnight at room temperature (meaning *cold* in Scotland). Next morning stir *with a wooden spoon* and combine with second-day ingredients. Mix well. Allow to stand 1 hour in *warm* kitchen, stirring from time to time. Pack in 2 large pudding molds. Place over the top of each mold a piece of wet cheesecloth dusted with flour and put lid on mold. Steam puddings for 5 hours. Take care to leave water level just under the lid at all times. Unmold puddings on heated platters.

Garnish with sprig of holly on top.

Place 1 teaspoon honey in ladle. Fill with brandy. Set ablaze and pour over pudding. Serve with Honey Hard Sauce (see index) on the side.

Pudding may be steamed ahead of time, kept in refrigerator in the mold, and reheated on Christmas day.

Freeze in airtight container. Steam when re-serving, until thoroughly warm.

Note: When I made this pudding I used heather honey.

HONEY ALMOND SAUCE

1 tablespoon flour
⅛ teaspoon salt
½ cup unstrained orange
 juice, pits removed
½ cup honey
1½ tablespoons sweet butter
½ teaspoon grated orange
 rind

½ teaspoon grated lemon
 rind
⅓ cup blanched, shaved
 almonds
2 tablespoons Grand Marnier
½ teaspoon almond extract
¼ teaspoon vanilla extract

Blend thoroughly flour, salt, orange juice alternately with honey. When the blend is smooth, cook it over gentle heat, stirring constantly, until mixture coats the spoon. Remove from fire and stir in butter, grated rinds, and shaved almonds. Immediately before serving stir in flavoring—Grand Marnier, almond and vanilla extracts. Heat without boiling and serve.

Make in quantity. Store in small portions in airtight containers in freezer. Will keep 8 days in refrigerator.

Note: Good with blancmange, too.

TURKISH EKMEK KHADAYIFF WITH KAYMAK

4 cups water   1 pint honey
juice of 2 lemons   8 Holland rusks

Steam rusks with lemon juice and water. When they have puffed out, put them in a flat round pan. Pour honey over them and bake 45 minutes at 350°F—or until brown.

Serve with Kaymak (below).

KAYMAK

4 cups whipping cream

Boil whipping cream very slowly. With a ladle lift cream out of saucepan and pour back from shoulder height until bubbles start rising. Keep this up from ½ to 1 hour. Remove from fire, but let cream remain in warm place for 2 hours. Then set in refrigerator for 8 hours. Remove bubbles that have set and discard them. Pour Kaymak over Ekmek Khadayiff.

Note: The famous chef, Tocatlian, concocted this delectable sweet in honor of Empress Eugénie of France. For Her Majesty's enjoyment he created the "bubbles of cream"—Kaymak

HONEY SPONGE LEMON PUDDING

1½ tablespoons butter
¾ cup strained honey
2½ tablespoons flour
¼ teaspoon salt
3 egg yolks, beaten
3 egg whites, beaten stiff

3 tablespoons lemon juice,
  mixed with grated rind
  of 1 lemon
1¼ cups cold buttermilk
2 or 3 drops lemon extract

Cream butter until light. Gradually work in strained honey and when thoroughly blended, beat in flour and salt alternately with egg yolks. Beat again for about ½ minute, adding, while beating, lemon juice alternately with cold buttermilk. When thoroughly blended, fold in egg whites, beaten with lemon extract. Pour into 6 custard cups. Place these in a pan of hot water and bake in a moderate oven (325–350°F) until delicately browned and custard is set. Chill well before serving.

Serves 6.

Will keep 24 hours in refrigerator.

SCOTCH HONEY PUDDING

12 ounces flour
6 ounces finely chopped beef
  suet
1 teaspoon baking powder

1 cup heather honey, slightly
  warmed
pinch of salt
Honey Cream Sauce II

Mix flour, suet, baking powder, and salt to a stiff paste with a little cold water. Roll out to the size of bowl. Put in a layer of paste and a layer of honey alternately. Tie firmly down and boil for two hours. Serve with Honey Cream Sauce II (see index).

Makes 4 generous portions.

HONEY CREAM SAUCE II

½ cup strained honey
½ cup light cream
2 tablespoons butter

2 tablespoons rum or
   curaçao or
1 tablespoon each curaçao
   and chartreuse

Combine honey, cream, and butter in saucepan and cook over
a medium flame for 10 minutes, or until a smooth syrup forms.
Beat in rum or curaçao and serve hot.

HONEY ORANGE SAUCE

2 tablespoons cornstarch
¼ cup honey
1 cup orange juice

½ cup raisins, cooked until
   plump and drained

Blend cornstarch and honey. Stir in orange juice. Cook over
low heat until mixture thickens, stirring all the time. Add
raisins. Continue cooking until sauce is clear. Serve hot over
cake or gingerbread.

HONEY CHEESE PIE

Dough for 2 Pies

1¼ cups flour
¼ teaspoon salt
¼ teaspoon double-acting
   baking powder

¼ cup butter
¼ cup margarine
4 tablespoons ice water
   (approximately)

Sift flour, salt, and baking powder. Cut butter and margarine
in pea-size pieces on top of the flour. Toss lightly, adding water slowly, just enough to bind together. Turn out on waxed

paper. Gather, handling as little as possible, into a square pile. Put another piece of waxed paper on top and pound with rolling pin to flatten. Roll into oblong piece ½-inch thick. Remove top paper. Fold in thirds and roll out again under paper. Repeat twice. Then cut dough into equal parts. Roll as thin as possible from center to edges between waxed paper, keeping it round. Remove top paper. Invert second paper with crust dough over 8-inch pie plate. Gently pull off paper. Prick with fork. Crimp edges. Pour in filling.

Piecrust freezes very well in airtight container or may be kept 24 hours in refrigerator.

Filling for 1 Pie

9 ounces cream cheese (large package)
½ cup strained honey
3 eggs, slightly beaten
¼ teaspoon salt
1½ cups milk
juice and grated rind of ½ lemon
nutmeg

Cream cheese until soft. Combine honey, eggs, salt, and milk. Add gradually to cheese, mixing until blended. Add lemon juice and rind. Pour filling into pastry-lined pie pan. Sprinkle with nutmeg. Bake in hot oven (450°F) 10 minutes, reduce temperature to slow (325°F), and bake ½ hour longer, or until knife inserted in center of filling comes out clean. Cool.

Serves 6.

Will keep 24 hours in refrigerator. Freeze in airtight container. To serve, thaw for 8 hours in refrigerator.

HONEY PEACH PIE

your favorite recipe for pie crust
sliced fresh peaches
1 tablespoon quick-cooking tapioca
⅓ cup honey

Line an 8-inch pie pan with pastry. Fill with sliced peaches. Sprinkle peaches with quick-cooking tapioca. Dribble honey on it. Lay twisted strips of pastry across the top. Fasten well at edges. Bake in hot oven (425°F) until delicately browned, about 35 to 40 minutes.

Serves 6.

YOGURT PIE

1 cup yogurt	1 tablespoon honey
9 ounces or 1 large package cream cheese	½ teaspoon vanilla extract
	baked pie shell (see index)

Mix yogurt, cream cheese, honey, and vanilla and whip to consistency of heavy whipped cream. Pour into pie shell and refrigerate until set.

Serves 6

OLD-FASHIONED HONEY PIE

your favorite recipe for pie crust	4 egg whites, beaten to moist peaks
4 egg yolks	½ cup brown sugar, packed
¾ cup buckwheat or dark honey	1 teaspoon nutmeg

Beat egg yolks and honey until light and foamy. Add nutmeg and brown sugar and continue beating. Fold in egg whites. Bake in moderate oven (350°F) for 1 hour. Open oven door partially and leave in oven until cool.

Serves 6.

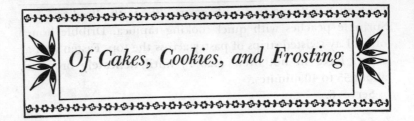

Of Cakes, Cookies, and Frosting

"And Abraham hastened into the tent unto Sarah, and said, Make ready quickly three measures of fine meal and honey, knead it, and make cakes upon the hearth."

GENESIS XVIII, 6

*B*AKING with honey is as old as Genesis. For a very long time in history honey recipes were limited to three ingredients—flour, fruit, and honey. The Egyptians, who used nothing but honey as sweetening, paid more attention to the fancy shapes of birds and scarabs into which they molded their cakes than to their flavor and lightness. The Athenians far surpassed them as pastry cooks. Their sweet cakes of honey, milk, fruit, and sesame flour were renowned all over the Mediterranean world. After the conquest of Greece it became fashionable for Roman epicures to finish their meals with spiral-shaped mixtures of flour and honey, baked, then soaked in wine, and sprinkled with great quantities of poppy seed. Thus, dessert was born.

Cakes made with honey were prescribed offerings to the gods of many lands. Even in China, the native land of the sugar cane, the legends of the River Yangtze speak of a Flood God who came rolling out of the fog and angrily refused human sacrifice, but who would be appeased by the gift of a large honey cake baked in the shape of a man.

During the Middle Ages, spiced honey cakes were introduced to Northern Europe from the Near East via the Russian
market of Nizhni Novgorod, which was then the crossroad of
the world.

By A.D. 1350, many cities had Bakers' Guilds specializing in
the exclusive manufacture of various types of honey cakes.
The Nuremberg Lebkuchen Bakers' Guild was one of the
earliest and most famous. Around Bruges, Ghent, and Amster-
dam, once the most important ports of the Occident, there are
still, in the meandering streets of the towns, shops that sell
nothing but honey cakes in untold varieties. The shopkeeper,
usually an old woman in a black shawl, will help you make
your selection from the fragrant shelves and then graciously
suggest that she cut the crust off the *pain d'épices* before
weighing it, for the crust on *pain d'épices* is apt to be chewy,
and few people like it. Holland, Italy, and France have their
traditional honey cakes, and Russia has *vertuta,* a pastry roll
stuffed with honey, nuts, and spices.

Mediæval recipes are excellent and many have been adapted
for modern usage by toning down the large quantities of mace,
cardamon, ginger, and poppy seed of which our forefathers
were so fond.

Many of these ancient cakes call for a proportionately large
amount of honey. Due to the faculty honey has of retaining
and absorbing external moisture it is impossible to give ac-
curate quantities of flour to be used: depending on dry or wet
weather, and on the texture and stickiness of honey itself, different quantities of flour must be used with the honey to make
doughs of the right consistency. The modern cook, trained to
use step-by-step directions and foolproof measurements may
find this somewhat baffling. Experience will soon overcome
that feeling. Accuracy is not quite so important in these old-
fashioned cakes as in our modern ones.

You may want to do a little experimenting yourself and try
your hand at adapting some of your personal sugar recipes to

honey cookery. When substituting honey for sugar in any cake using more than ½ cup of sugar, reduce liquids in recipe by ¼ cup and add ½ teaspoon baking soda per cup of honey. It is also good to know that honey and molasses are interchangeable in any recipe.

In the recipes in this book, follow the general rules for baking:

1. Always preheat oven to given temperature. If your range lacks thermostatic control, it might be wise to invest in an oven thermometer.
2. Measure accurately. To measure honey without trouble, use a cup which has been greased beforehand—the honey rolls out of it.
3. Have all ingredients at room temperature unless otherwise stated.
4. If you use an electric beater *do not overbeat*. It is bad for texture.
5. Use ingredients in the order listed in recipe. When doubling a recipe, select two identical pans. That way baking time does not have to be increased.
6. Handle finished product as stipulated in the recipe.

HOW TO FREEZE BAKED GOODS MADE WITH HONEY

Bread or Rolls. Bake and cool completely. Wrap in freezer paper and freeze. Thaw, when ready to use, in wrapper in a slow oven (300°F) from 20 to 30 minutes.

Baked Cakes. Freeze without frosting for best results. Wrap each layer, when cold, separately in freezer paper or foil. When ready to use, thaw in sealed package for 10 minutes in a slow oven (300°F) or 3 hours at room temperature.

Frosted Cakes. Freeze without packaging, wrap when stiff. Do not unwrap for thawing. Butter creams and uncooked frosting freeze best.

Cookies. Pack in cardboard boxes between layers of waxed paper. Thaw at room temperature.

Unbaked Cookie Roll. Wrap in waxed paper and freeze. Thaw enough to slice at room temperature and bake as a fresh product.

Drop Cookies, Unbaked. Freeze on cookie sheet, store in boxes when frozen. When ready to use, replace on cookie sheet and bake as fresh product.

HANDY HELPERS FOR BAKERS

Molds, ring molds, and good heavy baking pans.
Mortar and pestle for spices. Order the common glass kind
   through your local druggist.
Stainless steel or Pyrex bowls.
At least 2 one-cup measuring cups and 1 four-cup measuring
   cup.
Aluminum or plastic measuring spoon.
Slotted stainless steel mixing spoon.
Good potholders or oven mitts.
One-cup flour sifter.
1 large flour sifter.
Double Boiler—a quart size will be more useful than a small
   one.
Baking sheets with edges.
Rolling pins: plain and embossed.
Pastry board.
Wire or straw racks for cooling cakes and cookies.
Pie plates (aluminum).
Oblong Pyrex baking dish.

EQUIVALENT MEASURES

BUTTER

1 ounce = 2 tablespoons

(formerly known as "butter size of walnut")

1 pound = 2 cups

FLOUR

1 ounce = 3 to 4 tablespoons

4 ounces (sifted) = 1 cup

SUGAR

5 ounces (granulated) = 1 cup

CONTAINERS

1 No. 1 can = 1⅓ cups   1 No. 2 can = 2½ cups

1 No. 2½ can = 3½ cups   1 No. 3 can = 4 cups

1 kilogram = 2.2 pounds   28 grams = 1 ounce

115 grams = ¼ pound

BELGIAN COUQUE DE DINANT

[start 2 days ahead]

2 cups buckwheat honey,   about 4 cups flour, more or
   warm   less

[Absorbency of honey varies with quality and weather conditions. It is therefore impossible to give exact measurements of flour.]

Put honey in mixing bowl. Gradually work in as much flour as honey will hold to make a stiff paste. Roll out between 2 sheets of waxed paper to ½-inch thickness. Cover. Allow to stand two days at room temperature; it will rise slightly; then cut out with the edge of a 6-inch bowl. If you wish, use floured embossed rolling pin to press in designs, or old wooden gingerbread molds. Bake in slow oven (300°F) for 25 minutes or until light-brown, almost yellow.

Will keep indefinitely in airtight container.

Makes 8 to 10 cakes.

Note: These cakes are hard and should be dunked when eaten. They have been a specialty of the city of Dinant since the Middle Ages. They are, upon analysis, the closest thing to the Biblical cake of flour and honey. Yemenites and Samaritans of Israel still make similar ones today, as do North African tribesmen. The cereal from which the flour is ground may vary from country to country, but this cake is universal wherever honey and cereals are to be found.

Progress, and more sophisticated palate-teasers, have displaced this simple sweet. The Couque, however, has persisted in the Belgian city of Dinant because of the coppersmiths. In the thirteenth century they made artistic molds, copies of which are sold to tourist and townsman alike in Dinant.

FRENCH COUQUE DE REIMS

4 cups flour, more or less
¾ cup honey, lukewarm
1 cup dark-brown sugar, packed
½ teaspoon cinnamon
½ teaspoon ground aniseed
1 teaspoon baking soda
¾ cup hot water
a little milk
colored sugar seeds

[*Absorbency of honey varies with quality and weather conditions. It is therefore impossible to give exact measurements of flour in this recipe.*]

Dissolve honey in hot water. Sift flour and spices gradually into liquid. Blend well and beat. Work in baking soda until dough is rather stiff. Roll out to ¼ inch. Cut out in 2- to 3-inch circles. Brush with milk. Sprinkle your family's initial in sugar confetti on Couques and bake in medium hot oven (375°F) 12 to 15 minutes, or until done.

Will keep indefinitely in airtight container.

Note: This cooky, chewy and dark-brown, has been sold since time immemorial at all French country fairs.

ITALIAN PANFORTE FROM SIENA

FIRST STEP

¼ pound blanched almonds
¼ pound lightly toasted
   hazelnuts
⅓ cup cocoa
1½ teaspoons cinnamon
¼ teaspoon allspice
½ cup cake flour

¾ cup candied orange peel,
   chopped
¾ cup candied citron,
   chopped
¾ cup candied lemon peel,
   chopped

SECOND STEP

¾ cup honey
¾ cup sugar

½ cup confectioner's (powdered) sugar
1 tablespoon cinnamon

Blend first mixture. Put honey and sugar in large saucepan and bring to hard-ball stage (240°F on candy thermometer). Add first mixture to this and blend very well. Line 9-inch spring-form pan with waxed paper and pour in mixture. Bake in very slow oven (300°F) for 30 minutes. Release spring. Then remove side and bottom. Sprinkle with confectioner's sugar and cinnamon while warm. Cool. Wrap in foil. Will keep indefinitely in airtight container. Has the appearance of an overlarge hard cookie.

Note: Traditionally baked for the Palio, the re-enactment of mediæval jockey races held every summer among the various guilds of the city of Siena in Italy.

LAFAYETTE'S OWN GINGERBREAD
[as given by his cook to a French family]

1½ pounds flour, stone
   ground
½ pound sweet butter
½ pound brown sugar
1 cup honey
4 ounces ginger
2 sticks cinnamon, pounded

3 ounces allspice
cloves, pounded
dried lemon peel, pounded
5 eggs
pearl ash (in other words,
   refined potash home-
   made from wood ashes)

The above version is too spicy for modern palates, but for a wonderful cake, I suggest:

1 cup sweet butter
1 cup dark-brown sugar,
   packed
1 cup honey
2 tablespoons ginger

1 tablespoon cinnamon
½ tablespoon allspice
½ tablespoon powdered
   cloves
3 cups stone-ground flour

Cream butter and sugar. Add honey. Cream until light and foamy. Add spices. Add eggs and flour alternately. Add lemon rind last. Beat for 2 minutes in blender, or 300 strokes. Bake in heavy iron pan or skillet in moderate oven (375°F) for 30 to 35 minutes, or until done.
   Freezes very well.

SOFT GINGERBREAD

1 teaspoon each of cinnamon,   ¾ cup molasses
   nutmeg, cloves, baking   ¾ cup granulated honey
   powder, baking soda   ¾ cup sifted flour
¾ cup boiling water

Mix all ingredients together. Beat 2 minutes or 300 strokes.
Bake in slow oven (350°F) and serve with honey-sweetened
baked apple and cream.
   Freezes very well.

GINGERBREAD

½ cup shortening   1 teaspoon nutmeg
1 cup brown sugar, packed   2 teaspoons baking soda
2 eggs   ½ teaspoon salt
1 teaspoon grated lemon   1½ teaspoons ginger
   rind   ½ cup boiling water
2 cups sifted all-purpose   ½ cup honey
   flour

Cream shortening and sugar. Beat in eggs, one at a time. Add
grated lemon rind. Resift flour with nutmeg, soda, salt, and
ginger. Combine, in a separate bowl, boiling water and honey.
Add sifted and liquid ingredients alternately to butter mixture. Beat batter after each addition until ingredients are
blended. Bake in a buttered 8 x 11-inch pan in a moderate
oven (350°F) for about 40 minutes.
   Freezes very well.

MENNONITE APPLESAUCE GINGERBREAD

⅓ cup butter
½ cup brown sugar, packed
½ cup honey
1 egg
1¾ cups all-purpose flour
   sifted with
  ½ teaspoon salt
  1 teaspoon double-acting
    baking powder

½ teaspoon baking soda
1½ teaspoons powdered
   ginger
1 teaspoon cinnamon
2 cups sliced apples
¾ cup sour milk or buttermilk

Cream butter and add sugar. Add beaten egg and honey and continue to beat until well blended. Add sifted flour mixture alternately with sour milk. Beat thoroughly after each addition. Cover bottom of buttered 8 x 10 x 1¼-inch pan with slices of apple. Pour batter over apples. Bake for 40 to 45 minutes, or until done, at 350°F.

Freezes very well.

SUGARLESS CHOCOLATE HONEY CAKE

1¾ cups sifted flour
1 teaspoon baking soda
¾ teaspoon salt
½ cup butter
½ teaspoon almond extract
⅔ cup honey

7 ounces semi-sweet chocolate
2 eggs
⅔ cup water
½ cup chopped nut meats

Resift flour with soda and salt. Beat butter until creamy. Add flavoring. Beat honey in gradually. Melt chocolate over hot water and beat in gradually. Beat eggs in one at a time. Stir

in sifted ingredients in about 3 parts alternately with water.
Add chopped nut meats. Bake in two 8-inch layer pans in
moderate oven (350°F) for about 30 minutes. Freezes very well.
When the cake is cool or thawed, spread it with Sugarless
Chocolate Icing (below).

SUGARLESS CHOCOLATE ICING

3½ ounces chocolate morsels   ⅓ cup honey
2 egg whites   ½ teaspoon vanilla
⅛ teaspoon salt

Melt chocolate over hot water, cool to lukewarm. Beat egg
whites and salt until stiff but not dry. Add honey gradually,
beating constantly. Beat in chocolate. Add vanilla. Beat mixture until it is a good consistency to spread.

HONEY ORANGE CAKE

½ cup shortening   ¼ teaspoon salt
½ cup granulated sugar   ½ cup finely shredded
½ cup honey   orange peel
1 egg   ¼ cup orange juice
2 cups all-purpose flour   1 teaspoon grated lemon
2 teaspoons double-acting   rind or
   baking powder   1 teaspoon lemon flavoring
½ teaspoon baking soda

Cream shortening. Add sugar gradually, creaming until light
and fluffy. Add honey, beating until smooth. Beat in egg. Sift
together dry ingredients three times. Add orange peel. Combine orange juice and lemon rind or flavoring. Add dry ingredients alternately with orange juice to creamed mixture be-

ginning and ending with flour mixture. Spread in well-greased square cake pan. The mixture is quite thick. Bake in moderate oven (350°F) about 45 to 60 minutes. Allow to stand 7 or 8 minutes before removing cake from pan. Serve with Honey Orange Sauce (below).

HONEY ORANGE SAUCE

½ cup orange juice ⅓ cup honey

Blend orange juice with honey. Pour over the warm, or cold, cake or serve separately.

BRAZILIAN CAKE

½ cup honey
1 stick (¼ pound) soft
    butter
2 egg yolks
1 teaspoon baking soda
1¼ teaspoon salt
1½ cups sifted cake flour

1 teaspoon double-acting
    baking powder
3 egg whites, beaten
1 glass currant jelly
1 cup shaved Brazil nuts
    or almonds

Cream honey and butter until light yellow. Add egg yolks. Beat. Reserve. Sift cake flour, salt, baking powder on piece of waxed paper. Mix in, a little at a time, honey, butter, egg mixture until smooth. Fold in egg whites. Pour in well-buttered loaf pan. Bake in preheated hot oven (375°F) for ½ hour or until done. Cool on a rack. Then spread cake with currant jelly. Sprinkle top and sides generously with shaved Brazil nuts.

Makes 1 tea loaf.

Freezes very well.

Note: To slice Brazil nuts, cover them with cold water and bring slowly to a boil. Simmer 2 minutes. They will shave in slices on the grater.

HONEY NOUGAT FROSTING

2 egg whites, unbeaten
1 cup granulated sugar
4 tablespoons cold water
2 tablespoons white corn syrup
2 tablespoons strained honey

¼ teaspoon cream of tartar
⅛ teaspoon salt
½ teaspoon vanilla extract
½ cup chopped nuts (reserve)

Combine all ingredients, except nuts, in top of double boiler. Place over rapidly boiling water and beat constantly for 7 minutes with hand beater or electric beater. Fold in the nuts.

Keeps well, even in the summer.

TRIPLE SEED CAKE

3 cups sifted flour
2½ teaspoons double-acting baking powder
½ teaspoon baking soda
¾ teaspoon nutmeg
1 teaspoon salt
⅔ cup butter
1 cup granulated sugar
1 cup honey

4 eggs
2 tablespoons grated orange rind
1 tablespoon grated lemon rind
1 cup milk
1 tablespoon caraway seed
1 tablespoon poppy seed
1 tablespoon aniseed

Sift flour, baking powder, baking soda, nutmeg, and salt together. Blend together butter, sugar, and honey. Add unbeaten eggs, one at a time. Beat 1 minute after each is added. Blend in grated orange and lemon rind; mix thoroughly. Add milk alternately with dry ingredients to creamed mixture, beginning and ending with dry ingredients. Blend thoroughly after each addition. Spread ¼ of batter in 10-inch tube pan, well greased and lightly floured on bottom only. Sprinkle with caraway seed. Alternate remaining batter with poppy seed and aniseed, ending with batter on top. Bake in moderate oven (350°F) 75 to 80 minutes. Let cool in pan 15 minutes before turning out. Glaze with Fruit Juice Glaze (below) while slightly warm.

FRUIT JUICE GLAZE

1¼ cups confectioner's sugar, sifted
2 tablespoons orange juice

1 teaspoon lemon juice

Combine sifted confectioner's sugar, orange juice, and lemon juice. Beat until well blended.

A KIND OF BABA AU RHUM

1 package dry yeast diluted in ¼ cup lukewarm water
2 cups sifted flour
½ cup honey

½ cup butter
½ teaspoon salt
1 tablespoon grated lemon rind
3 eggs, well beaten

Add 1 tablespoon honey to ½ cup flour. Beat until smooth. Add yeast. Cover and let rise in warm place (80 to 85°F) until doubled in bulk, about 1 hour. Cream butter, add remaining honey gradually. Cream until light and fluffy. Add salt, lemon rind, and eggs and beat until smooth. Stir in the remaining flour. Add to yeast mixture. Beat 15 minutes by hand or 5 minutes by electric mixer. Pour in buttered metal ring of 1½- to 2-quart capacity. Cover and let rise until doubled in bulk, about 1 hour. Bake in moderate oven (350°F) 40 to 50 minutes. Remove from oven. Prick top with tines of sharp fork. Turn out of pan and place cake (inverted) in pie plate. Pour Baba Sauce (see below) over top and sides, then brush with Apricot Glaze (below). Allow cake to stand until most of the Baba Sauce is absorbed before serving.

Makes one 9-inch cake. Can be made 24 hours ahead.

BABA SAUCE

1 cup honey   ½ cup rum
1½ cups tea, clear and strong

Boil honey and tea 5 minutes. Cool. Add rum.

APRICOT GLAZE

¼ pound apricots   sugar

Soak apricots overnight in just enough water to cover. Press through sieve. Measure equal parts pulp and sugar. Boil together 5 minutes, stirring constantly.

DUTCH HONEY CAKE

½ cup dark-brown sugar,   ½ teaspoon double-acting
    packed   baking powder
1 egg   ⅓ teaspoon each of ground
½ cup honey   black pepper, allspice,
3 tablespoons molasses,   nutmeg, cinnamon
    brown   2 tablespoons butter, melted
1 teaspoon baking soda   1½ cups flour, sifted

Beat egg with sugar in a bowl. Add honey and molasses. Dilute soda in a little water; add this, melted butter, and spices to mixture in bowl. Beat well, all together. Then incorporate flour gradually.

Thoroughly grease a loaf pan and pour mixture in it up to two-thirds of edge. Bake in 350°F oven for about 30 minutes. To make sure honey cake is baked enough, run knife blade through center. Blade should come out clean. Allow to stand in pan 5 minutes. Then remove and cool on wire rack.

Will keep 8 days.

SPRITZKUCHEN

These are left-over squares of Honey Cake layered with raspberry jam and topped with a butter chocolate icing (page 133).

Will keep 8 days.

LEKACH

[traditional Jewish honey cake]

3½ cups sifted cake flour
1½ teaspoons double-acting
   baking powder
1 teaspoon baking soda
1 cup granulated sugar
6 eggs, well beaten
1 cup honey
2 tablespoons vegetable oil

½ cup raisins
½ cup chopped nuts
¼ cup chopped citron
½ teaspoon allspice
½ teaspoon cinnamon
½ teaspoon ground cloves
2 tablespoons brandy

Mix and sift flour, baking powder, and baking soda. Add sugar gradually to eggs and beat until light. Stir in honey and oil. Add raisins, nuts, citron, allspice, cinnamon, cloves, and brandy. Mix in flour, beating vigorously. Pour into cake pan lined with greased paper. Bake in slow oven (300° F) 1 hour. Invert pan until cake is cold.

SCRIPTURE CAKE

[a fine fruit cake]

Judges v, 25	Exodus xvi, 31
Jeremiah vi, 20	Genesis xxiv, 17
Isaiah x, 14	1 Kings iv, 22
1 Samuel xxx, 12	Leviticus ii, 13
1 Samuel xxx, 12	Amos iv, 5
Genesis xliii, 11	Kings x, 10

Follow Solomon's advice for making good boys (Proverbs xxiii, 14) and you will have a good cake. Amen.

This type of recipe was the fashion at sewing bees and quilting parties *circa* 1830, and perhaps earlier. The recipes were given by the originator as a guessing game which genteelly tested the guest's knowledge of the Bible, her ability as a cook, and prevented the virtuous gathering from indulging in idle gossip. The little boys passed the sliced cake, and it wasn't always as good as this one, which has a rich mellow taste and an intriguing texture caused by the addition of figs. With a few bastings of brandy or rum it makes a very good holiday cake. Solomon's advice is, of course: beat often with the rod.

Translated into modern cookery terms, here is how the recipe reads:

1 cup butter	3½ cups sifted flour
3 cups granulated sugar	⅛ teaspoon salt
6 eggs	4 teaspoons double-acting
2 cups raisins	baking powder
2 cups figs	¼ teaspoon each of ground
1 cup almonds	cloves, powdered cinna-
¼ cup honey	mon, mace, nutmeg
¾ cup water	⅛ teaspoon allspice

Blend all ingredients and beat well by hand or in the mixer. Pour into buttered and lightly floured angel-cake pan. Bake at medium temperature (300°F) for 3 hours, or until cake needle shows clean.

Improves by standing 24 hours or by freezing.

ORANGE HONEY SHORTCAKE

2 cups flour
4 teaspoons double-acting
   baking powder
½ teaspoon salt
1 tablespoon honey

1 egg beaten with
¾ cup top milk or cream
¼ cup butter
4 cups orange sections

Have butter at room temperature. Mix dry ingredients and sift twice. Work in butter with fingertips. Add egg and milk. Toss on waxed paper. Pat into shape. Cover with another sheet of paper. Roll out and bake on buttered cookie-sheet for 12 to 18 minutes (depending on size) in hot oven (450°F). Split while warm and place 4 cups orange sections between layers and on top. Serve with Honey Orange Sauce (see index).

HONEY SPICE CAKE

2 cups sifted flour
2¾ teaspoons double-acting
   baking powder
½ teaspoon salt
1 to 2 teaspoons cinnamon
½ teaspoon cloves
½ teaspoon freshly grated
   nutmeg

⅔ cup butter
½ cup granulated sugar
½ cup honey
½ teaspoon vanilla
3 eggs
¼ cup milk

Resift flour with baking powder, salt, cinnamon, cloves, and nutmeg. Beat butter until soft. Gradually add sugar and cream until fluffy. Add honey in 3 parts, beating well after each addition. Beat in ¼ of sifted ingredients and vanilla. Beat eggs until thick and frothy, then add to batter. Add remaining sifted ingredients in 3 parts alternately with milk. Beat batter after each addition. Bake cake in buttered tube pan in a slow oven (325°F) for about 65 minutes.

Freezes well.

SPICY OATMEAL CAKES

2 eggs
1½ cups granulated sugar
1½ cups milk
½ cup butter
¼ cup quick-cooking oatmeal
3 tablespoons honey

2 cups sifted flour
2 teaspoons double-acting
   baking powder
1 teaspoon cinnamon
¼ teaspoon each of cloves
   and nutmeg

Blend unbeaten eggs and sugar in large saucepan. Add milk and butter and cook over high heat, stirring occasionally, until mixture boils. Cool to lukewarm. Stir in oatmeal and honey. Add (all at once) the flour, baking powder, cinnamon, cloves, and nutmeg. Blend, then beat 1 minute, 150 strokes. Put batter in 18 cupcake pans, lined with paper baking cups—fill ½ to ⅔ full. Bake in moderate oven (350°F) 25 to 30 minutes. Cool and frost with Orange Honey Frosting (see index).

Freezes well.

EASY FLUFFY HONEY FROSTING

1 egg white
dash of salt

½ cup honey

Beat egg white with salt until stiff enough to hold up in peaks, but not dry. Pour honey in fine stream over egg white, beating constantly until frosting holds its shape. (Beat about 2½ minutes with electric mixer, or about 4 minutes by hand.)

Makes frosting to cover tops of two 8-inch layer cakes.

SANDWICH SPICE CAKE

KEEP SEPARATELY

3 tablespoons honey	1 teaspoon cinnamon
1 tablespoon allspice	1 cup chopped floured raisins
1 teaspoon cloves	

2 cups granulated sugar	2 teaspoons double-acting
½ cup butter	baking powder
3 eggs, well beaten	1 teaspoon salt, scant
3¼ cups flour, sifted and	1 cup milk
sifted again with	1 teaspoon vanilla

Cream butter and sugar until almost white. Add eggs and salt. Mix in flour alternately with milk. Add vanilla. Butter and flour 3 layer-cake pans and pour ⅔ of batter into two pans. To the remaining batter add all the ingredients kept separately. Pour into third pan. Bake 30 minutes in moderate oven (350°F). Cover with Honey Nougat Frosting (see index).

Note: I have made a similar cake very successfully in a short-cut way: use 2 packages of yellow cake-mix according to directions, thus doubling the batter. Pour 2 equal parts in well-buttered layer-cake pans, reserving a third part, to which add spices.

Bake according to directions on package. Cover with Honey Nougat Frosting (see index).

PRESSURE COOKER GIFT CAKES

[make 4 days ahead; have 6 empty coffee cans handy]

4½ cups cake flour
1 teaspoon double-acting
   baking powder
1 teaspoon baking soda
½ teaspoon salt
1 teaspoon allspice
1 teaspoon ginger

1 cup seedless raisins
½ cup finely cut dates
½ cup butter
½ cup granulated sugar
2 eggs, well beaten
1 cup honey
1 cup top milk

Sift cake flour, baking powder, baking soda, salt, allspice, and ginger into a mixing bowl and combine, mixing well, with raisins and dates.

Cream butter until soft, light, and smooth; gradually add sugar, cream and beat well. Then add well-beaten eggs, and, when well blended, honey. Gradually add flour-fruit mixture and milk. Pour cake batter into greased cans, filling them only half full to allow for rising, and cover top of each can with 3 thicknesses of waxed paper. Pour 4 quarts hot water into canning-type pressure cooker; place cans on the rack, lock the cover on cooker, and steam with petcock open for 30 minutes, depending on size of cakes, then close petcock and cook 1 hour at 15 pounds pressure. Pour Royal Icing (below) on top of cakes after cooking and before putting on can lids, to help protect against mold.

ROYAL ICING

½ pound confectioner's
   (powdered) sugar

1 egg white, unbeaten
1 teaspoon lemon juice

Add sugar gradually to egg white, work together well with slotted spoon, until smooth. Add juice, stir, and spread quickly.

MY OWN GÂTEAU ROLLA

[start 2 days ahead]

MERINGUE LAYERS

4 egg whites, beaten stiff
½ cup sifted confectioner's
   (powdered) sugar
⅓ cup finely ground almonds
4 rounds wax paper the size
   of a layer-cake pan

Fold sugar and almonds alternately in beaten egg whites. Spread evenly on rounds of paper and bake 20 minutes at 250°F. Remove paper, turn the meringues, and continue to bake on other side for another 15 minutes, or until dry.

FILLING

2 egg whites, beaten till
   frothy
½ cup honey
2 tablespoons cocoa
1 cup softened sweet butter
¼ cup ground almonds
4 ounces semi-sweet chocolate, melted

In top of double boiler, over hot water, beat sugar, cocoa, butter, and chocolate with egg whites for 2 minutes, or 300 strokes. Fold in nuts. Remove from heat. Cool. When filling is firm, spread it on meringue layers and put them together, leaving top one plain. Make a lattice of waxed paper, arrange it on top of cake, and sift powdered sugar over cake to make a design. Remove paper. Allow cake to ripen 24 hours at room temperature before serving.

SPICY PUMPKIN CAKE

1 package Cup Cake Mix
1 egg
¼ cup honey
½ teaspoon cinnamon
½ teaspoon nutmeg
1 cup canned pumpkin
½ cup chopped nuts
½ cup finely chopped dates

Empty contents of package into bowl; add remaining ingredients, except dates and nuts, and blend. Beat 2 minutes. Stir in dates and nuts. Pour into 2 greased 8-inch layer-cake pans. Bake at 375°F (moderate oven) 25 to 30 minutes. Cool five minutes before removing from pans.

Cover with Orange Honey Frostings (see index).

A VERY QUICK HONEY CAKE

1 package Cup Cake Mix	½ teaspoon cinnamon
1 egg	¼ teaspoon mace (optional)
½ cup milk	½ cup chopped nuts (optional)
¼ cup honey	
½ teaspoon ginger	

Empty contents of package into bowl. Add remaining ingredients and blend. Beat 2 minutes or 300 strokes. Pour into greased 8-inch square pan. Bake at 350°F (moderate oven) 30 to 35 minutes. Cool five minutes before removing from pan.

Freezes very well.

WALNUT HONEY LOAF

1 teaspoon salt	½ cup granulated sugar
2½ cups sifted flour	½ cup walnuts, chopped
1 teaspoon baking soda	¼ cup shortening
1 cup honey	2 unbeaten egg yolks
1 cup milk	

Sift flour, baking soda, salt together.

Heat honey, milk, sugar in saucepan over medium heat, stirring constantly, until sugar is dissolved. Cool. Add walnuts, shortening, and egg yolks, beating and blending, and gradually add sifted mixture. Beat all together 2 minutes or 300 strokes. Turn into 9 x 5 x 3-inch pan which has been generously greased and lightly floured on the bottom only. Bake in slow oven (325°F) 5 to 8 minutes. Cool for 15 minutes.

Remove from pan and cool on wire rack.

Makes 1 loaf.

Freezes very well.

QUICK HONEY KUCHEN

BATTER

¾ cup sifted all-purpose flour
2½ teaspoons double-acting baking powder
¼ teaspoon salt
½ cup milk
¼ cup honey

1 egg, well beaten
3 tablespoons melted shortening
1½ cups wheat flakes or 1½ cups bran flakes

HONEY NUT TOPPING

4 tablespoons butter
4 tablespoons granulated sugar

4 tablespoons sifted all-purpose flour
4 tablespoons honey
½ cup chopped nuts

Sift flour with baking powder and salt. Combine milk, honey, egg and add to flour mixture. Add shortening, mixing only enough to combine. Fold in flakes. Pour into greased pan.

Make Honey Nut Topping: Cream butter. Add sugar, mixing well. Add flour and honey and beat until well mixed. Add nuts.

Sprinkle over batter. Bake in hot oven (400°F) until done (25 minutes).

Makes 1 square cake (8 x 8 x 2).

Freezes very well.

FRENCH GALETTE DE NARBONNE

2 cups milk   1 package dry yeast
1½ tablespoons butter   3 teaspoons honey
4 cups flour   3 eggs
9 tablespoons cream

Dissolve yeast in ¼ cup lukewarm water. Add yeast to milk.
Mix ingredients, add all to flour, and knead. Cover with a
little flour; let stand for 2 or 3 hours. Roll out thin and put in
3 well-buttered 6-inch pie plates. Scatter bits of butter, size of
½ walnut, on dough. Take 1 egg for each pie plate and mix
with 3 tablespoons cream to each egg. Beat well. Pour over
Galettes and bake at 375°F until slightly brown.
Serves 6.
Must be eaten fresh from the oven.

TURKISH BAKLAVA

4 cups cake flour sifted with   1 cup ground, blanched al-
½ teaspoon salt   monds
2 slightly beaten eggs mixed   1 cup skinned pistachio nuts
with   1 cup hot melted butter
2 tablespoons water

HONEY SYRUP

1 cup honey boiled with 1 cup
water to consistency of a
thick syrup

Sift flour and salt into mixing bowl. Make a well in the center
and pour in eggs beaten with water. Blend the eggs in the
dough with the fingertips and knead into smooth paste. Beat
dough with a rolling pin, or a rod, until it blisters. Divide into

30 to 40 tiny pieces and roll each of them as thin as paper between two sheets of waxed paper. Lay these dough leaves singly on boards sprinkled with cornstarch and let them dry out for 1 hour. Then place 3 or 4 pieces on top of each other in oblong baking pan and sprinkle each group with nuts. Continue making alternate layers of dough leaves and nuts until the pan is ¾ full to the top. Pour melted butter over pastry and bake in hot oven (450°F) for 20 minutes. When pastry comes out of the oven, pour Honey Syrup over it. Cool and then cut in 2-inch squares. Keeps indefinitely in airtight containers.

MY OWN SCHNEKEN

[start 1 day ahead]

1 package dry yeast
¼ cup lukewarm water
2½ cups all-purpose flour
½ cup butter
2 beaten eggs
½ cup honey
1 teaspoon salt
1 cup sour cream

1 tablespoon butter, separately
4 tablespoons honey
1 teaspoon cinnamon
⅔ cup chopped nuts
⅔ cup currants, soaked until plump

Dilute yeast in lukewarm water. Add melted butter, sugar, sour cream, eggs, salt, and flour to dissolved yeast. Mix well. Allow to stand in refrigerator overnight. Divide dough into two parts. Roll out on a lightly floured board to ¼ inch. Dot with butter. Sprinkle with nuts, currants, and cinnamon. Dribble some honey over surface. Roll up as a pancake. Cut into ½-inch slices. Place in a buttered pan, cut side down. Allow to rise in warm place until double in bulk, about 2 hours. Bake in moderate oven (350°F), about 45 minutes, or until light brown. Cool. Serve before Schneken are cold.

Freezes very well.

JEANNE OWEN'S HONEY TWIST COFFEE CAKE

1 cup milk	2 packages dry yeast
1 teaspoon salt	½ cup lukewarm water
6 tablespoons butter	2 eggs, well beaten
¼ cup honey	4 or 5 cups flour, sifted twice

Dissolve yeast in water. Scald milk. Add salt, butter, and honey. When mixture is lukewarm, add dissolved yeast and eggs. Beat in flour, enough to form a soft dough. Knead dough until smooth. Form it into a ball, place in well greased bowl. Cover and allow to rise until double in bulk. Form into a long roll, about 1 inch in diameter and coil roll into greased 9-inch cake pan, beginning at outer edge and rolling toward the center, covering bottom of pan.

Cover twist in the pan with Honey Topping (below).

HONEY TOPPING

¼ cup softened butter	3 tablespoons honey
⅔ cup confectioner's (pow-	½ cup chopped nuts (op-
dered) sugar	tional)
1 egg white	

Combine all ingredients and mix until smooth.

Sprinkle with chopped nuts (optional).

Freezes very well.

ORANGE MUFFINS

½ cup sifted unbleached	1 egg, well beaten
flour	¼ cup frozen orange juice,
½ teaspoon salt	diluted double strength
2 teaspoons double-acting	rind of 1 orange, grated
baking powder	½ cup honey
½ cup stone-ground whole-	3 tablespoons melted butter
wheat flour	

Sift flour, salt, and baking powder all together. Add whole-wheat flour and mix well. Mix egg, orange juice, rind, and honey together and add at once to flour. Don't stir more than to make the flour moist. Bake in well-buttered muffin pans at 400°F 15 to 20 minutes.

Freezes very well.

OLD-FASHIONED SPICY DOUGHNUTS

1¼ cups milk	1½ teaspoons cinnamon
¼ cup butter	¼ teaspoon nutmeg
½ teaspoon salt	⅛ teaspoon mace
1 package dry yeast	¾ cup honey
¼ cup lukewarm water	3 eggs
about 5 cups sifted flour	

Dissolve yeast in lukewarm water. Scald milk, add shortening and salt and cool to lukewarm. Add dissolved yeast and 2½ cups flour. Beat until smooth. Cover and let rise until bubbly. Mix spices with sugar and add to above. Add beaten eggs. Mix well. Add remaining flour to make a dough that can be kneaded. Knead until smooth. Cover and let rise until doubled in bulk. Roll out ½ inch thick and cut with floured doughnut cutter. Let rise on board until doubled in bulk. Fry in deep fat (375°F) 3 minutes, or until lightly browned, first on one side, then on the other. Drain on unglazed paper.

Makes about 3 dozen doughnuts.

HONEY SCONES

2 cups sifted all-purpose flour	4 tablespoons shortening
3 teaspoons double-acting baking powder	¼ cup currants (optional)
1 teaspoon salt	2 eggs
4 tablespoons honey	½ cup milk

Sift together flour, baking powder, salt, and honey. Cut in
shortening. Add currants, if desired. Beat together 1 whole egg
and 1 egg yolk, reserving 1 white for the tops. Add milk to
beaten eggs and add to dry ingredients. Stir only enough to
make dough hold together. Turn out on lightly floured board
and knead ½ minute. Roll out in circular shape to ½-inch
thickness. Cut into pie-shaped wedges. Brush tops with white
of egg. Bake in hot oven (425°F) 12 to 15 minutes. Serve with
honey.

Makes 10 to 12 scones.

MODERN VERSION OF MY GRANDMOTHER'S PAIN D'ÉPICES

[*Absorbency of honey being dependent on quality and atmospheric conditions, it is impossible to give exact proportions of flour in this recipe.*]

2½ cups all-purpose flour (more or less)
½ cup rye flour, more or less
2 teaspoons baking soda
3 teaspoons double-acting baking powder
1½ cups lukewarm honey
¼ teaspoon ground aniseed
¼ teaspoon ground coriander seed
½ teaspoon black pepper
½ teaspoon cinnamon
½ teaspoon powdered cloves
½ teaspoon mace
½ cup candied cherries
½ cup candied angelica
½ cup blanched almonds

Blend all together in a bowl until it makes a smooth semi-stiff
dough. Place in well-buttered square or rectangular bread pan.
Bake at 275°F for 3 hours without opening oven doors. Check
cake with pastry wire; if it comes clean out of center of cake,
it is done. If not, allow it to bake 15 minutes more. Brush tops

with slightly beaten egg white while hot and decorate rapidly with cherries, almonds, and angelica. Cools hard as a brick.

Allow cake to stand at least a day before use. Serve sliced, buttered, and made into a sandwich with a thin slice of white bread. Keeps indefinitely wrapped in foil.

Recipe may be doubled or tripled, if desired.

Note: We used to dunk these in *café au lait* for breakfast. Original recipe had a leaven made of milk, refined potash, and, of all things, 1 tablespoon grated floating soap. It tasted even better!

FRENCH SPICE BREAD

[pain d'épices]

1⅓ cups water
⅔ cup honey
⅔ cup brown sugar, packed
¼ cup rum
1 teaspoon baking soda
2 tablespoons double-acting
    baking powder

¼ teaspoon powdered ani-
    seed
⅛ teaspoon cinnamon
⅛ teaspoon salt
4 cups flour

Bring water to a boil. Dissolve brown sugar, honey, soda, and baking powder in it. Add spices and rum. Blend flour into this mixture making a stiff dough. Butter 2 bread pans. Pour in dough. Bake for 10 minutes at 425°F and 40 minutes at 375°F.

Makes 2 loaves.

Keeps indefinitely wrapped in foil.

HERB BREAD

2 cups milk	1 teaspoon nutmeg
4 tablespoons honey	4 teaspoons leaf sage
1 tablespoon salt	4 teaspoons caraway seed
1 package dry yeast	8 cups sifted flour
¼ cup lukewarm water	4 tablespoons butter, melted
2 eggs, well beaten	

Dilute yeast in lukewarm water. Scald milk. Add sugar and salt and cool to lukewarm. Add dissolved yeast. Add eggs, nutmeg, sage, caraway seed, honey, and half the flour. Beat until smooth. Add melted butter and remaining flour, or enough to make easily handled dough. Knead dough quickly and lightly until smooth and elastic. Place in buttered bowl, cover and set in warm place, free from draft. Let rise until doubled in bulk, about 2 hours. When light, divide into 2 equal portions and shape into loaves. Place in buttered loaf pans. Cover and let rise until doubled in bulk, about 1 hour. Bake in hot oven (425°F) for 15 minutes, then reduce to moderate (375°F) and bake 35 minutes longer.

Makes 2 loaves.

Freezes very well.

PEANUT BUTTER BREAD

2 cups flour	¼ teaspoon baking soda
4 teaspoons double-acting	¼ cup honey
baking powder	⅔ cup peanut butter
1 teaspoon salt	1¼ cups milk

Sift flour, baking powder, salt, and honey together. Add milk to peanut butter, blend well, and add to dry ingredients; beat thoroughly. The dough must be soft enough to take the shape of the pan. Bake in buttered loaf pan in moderate oven (350°F) 40 to 50 minutes.

Best when a day old.

Freezes very well.

FIG BREAD

¼ cup butter
¼ cup maple syrup
½ cup honey
1 egg
3 cups flour
1 cup ready-to-eat bran

3 teaspoons double-acting baking powder
¼ teaspoon baking soda
1 teaspoon salt
1½ cups milk
¾ cup chopped figs
½ cup chopped walnuts

Blend butter, syrup, and honey. Add beaten egg. Add bran. Sift flour, baking powder, soda, and salt. Add alternately with milk to first mixture. Fold in chopped figs and nuts, slightly floured. Bake in greased loaf pan in moderate oven (350°F) for about 1¼ hours.

Makes 1 loaf.

Freezes very well.

MILDRED KNOPF'S NUT BREAD

1½ cups whole-wheat flour, sifted
1½ cups white flour, sifted
4 tablespoons granulated sugar
6 tablespoons double-acting baking powder
¾ teaspoon salt
1 teaspoon baking soda

4 tablespoons honey
2 cups milk
¼ cup coarsely chopped pecans
¼ cup coarsely chopped walnuts
¼ cup coarsely chopped almonds

Pre-heat oven to 350°F. Resift both flours together 3 times with sugar, baking powder, salt, and baking soda. Place in a large mixing bowl. Make a well in the center and drop in honey and milk. Mix thoroughly so that the dry ingredients and the liquids are well blended. Beat pecans, walnuts, and almonds into the dough. Place in a greased loaf pan and bake in a 350°F oven for approximately 45 mintues, or until done.
Freezes very well.

Note: Toast this. Try spreading it with butter and cream cheese.

WHOLE-WHEAT FIG BREAD

1½ cups all-purpose flour, sifted

2 teaspoons double-acting baking powder

¼ cup brown sugar, packed

½ teaspoon salt

¾ teaspoon baking soda

1½ cups whole-wheat flour

1 egg, beaten

1½ cups milk

½ cup honey

2 tablespoons melted butter

1 cup chopped figs

½ cup chopped pecan meats

Resift flour with baking powder, brown sugar, salt, and baking soda. Add whole-wheat flour. Combine beaten egg, milk, honey, and melted butter and stir liquid into the sifted ingredients. Knead figs and pecan meats in well. Place dough in a greased 6 x 10-inch pan or in two 4 x 7-inch pans. Allow to rise for 20 minutes. Bake in a slow oven (350°F) for about 1 hour.
Freezes very well.

A BOSTON BROWN BREAD

2 cups buttermilk
2 teaspoons baking soda
4 tablespoons honey, dark
4 tablespoons dark-brown
    sugar

½ teaspoon salt
¼ cup butter
4 cups graham flour (approxi-
    mately)

Dissolve soda in buttermilk. Add honey, brown sugar, and salt. Beat in graham flour until it is a stiff batter. Add butter. Fill 2 coffee cans. Cover tightly. Steam for 3½ hours. Dry out for ½ hour in the oven.

Makes 2 loaves.

Note: Wrapped in tin foil these loaves will keep in refrigerator for a month. They freeze very well. Delicious when spread with Honey Butter (below).

HONEY BUTTER

½ cup butter   ¼ cup honey

Cream butter and beat honey into it.

May be made in quantity and stored in freezer in airtight containers.

Keeps 8 days in refrigerator.

Note: Good on hot puddings, waffles, and griddlecakes, as well as on Boston Brown Bread (see above).

MRS. LESLIE'S EIGHTEENTH-CENTURY GINGERBREAD NUTS

1 pound stone-ground flour, sifted
1 pound sweet butter
1 pound honey
1 ounce ginger

1 ounce allspice
3 ounces cloves
¼ ounce cinnamon
saleratus

MODERN INGREDIENTS

4 cups stone-ground flour, sifted
1 pound sweet butter
2 cups honey
1 teaspoon powdered ginger
½ teaspoon allspice

½ teaspoon cloves
½ teaspoon cinnamon
1 teaspoon baking soda
4 teaspoons double-acting baking powder

Mix and knead very thoroughly. Sprinkle additional flour in one hand, place small pieces of dough on it, roll in little round balls with both hands. Place on buttered pans. Bake in moderate oven.

Will keep indefinitely in airtight containers.

Note: The famous Mrs. Leslie was the oracle of eighteenth-century housewives—she wrote extensively on manners, home economics, and French and American cookery. On reading her cookbooks—no doubt intended for the great houses in this country—I was struck by the munificence of her recipes.

GINGERBREAD MEN

2¾ cups sifted cake flour
1 tablespoon baking soda
1 teaspoon ground cloves
4 teaspoons ground ginger
1 teaspoon ground cinnamon
½ teaspoon salt

1 egg, beaten
¼ teaspoon allspice
1 cup dark-brown sugar,
   packed
⅔ cup honey, dark
½ cup butter, soft

DECORATIONS
nuts   candied fruit   cinnamon drops

Sift flour, spices, soda, and baking powder into a bowl. In a second bowl combine egg, allspice, brown sugar, honey, and butter. Work with hands till mixture is homogenous. Divide into 3, or more, balls. Roll one ball out on floured board to ¼-inch thickness. Flour lightly on top and cut the gingerbread with special cutter. Repeat with other dough balls. Place gingerbread on buttered baking sheets. Make eyes and mouth and nose with candied fruit, nuts, and cinnamon drops. Bake in moderate oven (375°F) for about 12 minutes. To hang on Christmas tree, make a hole in the dough when it is baked but still hot and draw a string through it.

When thoroughly cold, store in airtight container.

PFEFFERNÜSSE

1 cup butter, soft
1½ cups honey, lukewarm
3 eggs, beaten
grated rind of 1 lemon
1 teaspoon ground pepper
1½ cups milk
5 cups flour
1 teaspoon salt

1 teaspoon baking soda
4 teaspoons double-acting
   baking powder
2 teaspoons ground carda-
   mon
confectioner's (powdered)
   sugar

Cream butter, eggs, and honey until almost white. Add lemon rind. Sift dry ingredients together and add them alternately with milk to creamed mixture. Drop, from tip of teaspoon, the size of a hazelnut on buttered baking sheet. Bake at 350°F for 15 minutes. Roll them immediately in confectioner's (powdered) sugar.

Makes about 50 cookies that will keep indefinitely.

FLEMISH PEPPERNOOTJES

[should ripen in airtight container 8 days before use]

1 cup honey, lukewarm
⅓ cup butter
1 teaspoon powdered mace
1 teaspoon powdered carda-
    mom
½ cup orange marmalade

1 teaspoon baking soda
4 teaspoons baking powder
1 teaspoon black pepper,
    ground
4 cups flour (more or less)

[Quantity of flour is dependent on absorbent quality of honey and cannot be given in exact measurement. Dough for this recipe must be stiff.]

Mix all ingredients and add flour gradually until dough is very stiff and will hold in little balls the size of a walnut. Drop ½ teaspoon orange marmalade in center of little ball and close over. Bake in medium oven (350°F) until brown—10 to 15 minutes.

Will keep indefinitely in airtight container.

MILDRED KNOPF'S LEBKUCHEN FOR CHRISTMAS
[start 2 days ahead]

2 tablespoons brandy
1 teaspoon ground carda-
  mom seed
½ tablespoon cinnamon
½ tablespoon powdered
  cloves
½ teaspoon mixture ginger,
  nutmeg, and white pep-
  per
4⅓ cups flour

2¼ cups (scant) strained
  honey
2 cups plus 3 tablespoons
  granulated sugar
2 eggs
1½ cups ground almonds
2 tablespoons butter
Royal Icing (see index)
wafer paper (optional)
sugar confetti
blanched whole almonds

Pour brandy over spices. Let stand overnight. Place flour in a
very large mixing bowl. Make a hollow in the center. In it
pour strained honey and sugar. Combine and let stand overnight.

Next day knead well. Add 2 eggs, one at a time, beating
until well blended. Knead well. Add almonds and knead again
very thoroughly.

[Preheat oven to 450°F]

Add brandy and spices to the dough, a little at a time, until
well blended. Butter generously two large cookie pans (with
edges). Line pan with wafer paper. Pour on dough and smooth
evenly all around with a knife moistened in water after each
stroke. Bake in a 450°F oven for 8 minutes. Turn oven down
to 400°F and bake for 30 to 45 minutes. When cooled, ice with
Royal Icing (see index). Sprinkle with sugar confetti and set
whole peeled almonds into the top. Cut into pieces 2 inches
by 4 inches and wrap in cellophane or waxed paper. These

cakes keep well for 3 weeks, but are at their best 1 week after baking.

Note: This ancient recipe originated at Nürnberg, Germany several centuries ago under the reign of Charles IV (1347–78). They were first made by a specially formed branch of the Bakers' Guild.

Wafer paper may be ordered from dealers listed under Bakers' supplies in the Classified Telephone Directory.

LEBKUCHEN II

[start 1 day ahead]

1 cup honey	soda, nutmeg, cloves
¾ cup brown sugar, packed	1 teaspoon cinnamon
1 tablespoon lemon juice	½ teaspoon crushed carda-
1 teaspoon grated lemon rind	mom seeds
1 egg, well beaten	⅓ cup chopped citron
2½ cups sifted flour	⅓ cup almonds, blanched
½ teaspoon each baking	and shredded

Add brown sugar, lemon juice, and grated lemon rind to honey. Beat in egg. Resift flour with soda, nutmeg, cloves, and cinnamon. Blend well and add cardamom seeds, citron, and almonds. Mix the dough well and let stand for 24 hours to ripen and mellow.

Preheat oven to 300°F.

Roll the dough into a sheet to ½-inch thickness and cut into rounds, hearts, or bars. Bake on a buttered baking sheet until very lightly browned, about 20 minutes.

Frost while still warm with an icing made of confectioner's sugar mixed to spreading consistency with cream and lemon juice. Decorate the soft icing with chopped nuts, blanched almond halves, or candied fruits, to taste.

Store a while before serving. Will keep indefinitely.

GERMAN HONEY CAKES

[start 2 days ahead]

3 cups honey
¼ cup butter
3 cups all-purpose flour
   (more or less), sifted with
2 teaspoons double-acting
   baking powder and
1½ teaspoons baking soda
¼ pound almonds, blanched
   and shredded

2 ounces chopped citron
1 cup granulated sugar
1½ tablespoons mixed spices
cinnamon, cloves, nutmeg,
   mace, allspice
2 tablespoons brandy
2 tablespoons water, wine, or
   rum

[Absorbency of honey being dependent on quality, it is impossible to give exact proportion of flour for this recipe.]

Heat honey slightly in a large saucepan. Add butter and melt. Sift flour. Add enough of it to make dough that will stick to the hands. Add almonds, citron, sugar, spices, and flavoring. Allow dough to ripen for 24 hours. Roll out dough between sheets of waxed paper and spread it to the thickness of ¼ inch in shallow buttered pans. Bake in a moderate oven (350°F). Cut cake into squares and ice them with Lemon Icing (page 118).

Will keep for weeks in a cool place. Will freeze very well also.

LEMON ICING

2 egg whites
⅛ teaspoon salt

grated rind and juice of 1
    lemon
confectioner's sugar

Beat egg whites until stiff. Sift and add sufficient confectioner's sugar, grated rind and juice of lemon to make the icing a good consistency to spread.

JEWISH TEIGLACH

DOUGH

2 cups sifted all-purpose flour
    (more or less)
¼ teaspoon ginger
¼ teaspoon salt

3 eggs, well beaten
2 tablespoons oil
chopped nut meats, raisins
    (optional)

SYRUP

1 cup honey
1 cup granulated sugar

2 teaspoons ginger

[*Absorbency of honey being dependent on quality and weather conditions, it is impossible to give exact proportion of flour in this recipe.*]

Mix and sift flour, ¼ teaspoon ginger, and salt. Gradually add flour mixture to eggs, oil, and, if desired, nuts and raisins, making a soft dough just stiff enough to handle. Divide dough into several parts. Roll each into a long sausage about ½ inch in diameter and cut into ½-inch pieces. Bring honey, sugar, and ginger to a rolling boil in a deep kettle to make syrup.

Drop pieces of dough into syrup, a few at a time, to prevent lowering of temperature. Cover and simmer ½ hour, shaking pan occasionally to prevent sticking. Turn gently from time to time with a wooden spoon. Cook until all Teiglach are golden brown and sound hollow when stirred. To test, break one open. If inside is crisp and dry, remove from heat. Add 2 tablespoons boiling water. Remove Teiglach to large platter with perforated spoon, placing them so that they do not touch each other. If desired, roll in sugar and chopped nuts. Cool and store like other cookies.

Note: These rather primitive cakes have been popular gifts for the Jewish New Year since time immemorial—they symbolize the sweetness of the year to come.

GREEK MELLOMAKARUNA

DOUGH

1 cup butter
¾ cup honey
juice of 1 orange
½ teaspoon vanilla

3 cups 2 tablespoons flour
½ teaspoon soda
1 teaspoon double-acting baking powder

SYRUP

2 cups sugar
1 cup honey

1½ cups water

Cream butter and honey until almost white. Add orange juice, cognac, and vanilla. Sift flour with soda and baking powder and add to creamed mixture gradually. Cut out heart shapes and bake on buttered cookie-sheet in moderate oven.

Make syrup by combining sugar, honey, and water. Dip baked cookies in this syrup. Sprinkle with chopped walnuts or almonds. Dry on rack. Store between layers of waxed paper.

SWISS LEKERLE

½ cup honey
½ cup granulated sugar
¼ cup slivered (on the
    grater) almonds
¼ teaspoon cinnamon
¼ teaspoon powdered cloves
⅛ teaspoon nutmeg

1 teaspoon baking soda
1 teaspoon double-acting
    baking powder
¼ cup mixed candied fruits
¼ cup cherry liqueur
2 cups flour

Place sugar and honey in a saucepan. Heat to a boil. Remove from heat. Add almonds, candied fruit, spices, and liqueur. Sift flour with baking soda and baking powder. Gradually blend with other ingredients. Beat 5 minutes. Roll to ¼ of an inch. Bake on a buttered cookie-sheet at 400°F. Divide while still warm, without going quite through them, into rectangles 2 x 2. Make a glaze by boiling ¼ pound sugar with ½ cup water until it bubbles. Spread with a brush in one stroke, never going over the same place.

Store between layers of waxed paper.

TURKISH KOURABIEDES

½ pound sweet butter
1 egg yolk
½ cup honey
2¾ cups sifted flour
¼ teaspoon baking soda

½ teaspoon double-acting
    baking powder
¼ teaspoon ground cloves
36 whole cloves (approxi-
    mately)

Beat butter and honey until almost white. Still beating, add egg yolk. Sift flour with baking soda, baking powder, and cloves. Fold into previous mixture. Preheat oven to 350°F. With fingertips shape cookies like small marshmallows. Insert 1 whole clove into center of cookie and place about 2 inches apart on ungreased sheet. Bake for about 15 minutes, or until they begin to brown. Remove from oven, roll in plenty of confectioner's sugar while hot.

Cool and store.

Makes about 36 cookies.

Freeze in airtight container if cookies must be kept over two weeks.

PEANUT-BUTTER COOKIES

FIRST MIXTURE

1 cup sifted flour	¼ teaspoon salt
½ teaspoon baking soda	

SECOND MIXTURE

½ cup shortening	½ cup peanut butter
½ cup honey	1 tablespoon water
½ cup granulated sugar	½ teaspoon vanilla
1 egg, unbeaten	

Sift together first mixture on waxed paper.

Put second mixture into a large bowl and beat 2 minutes, or 300 strokes. Add first mixture. Beat 1 minute, or 150 strokes. Drop by teaspoonfuls on greased cookie-sheet. Press lightly with a fork dipped in flour to flatten cookie and make ridged top. Bake at 325°F for 15 to 20 minutes.

Makes about 3½ dozen cookies which keep very well.

SUGARLESS BROWNIES

½ cup sifted flour	⅓ cup butter
½ teaspoon double-acting baking powder	2 eggs
¼ teaspoon salt	6 tablespoons honey
7 ounces semi-sweet chocolate	1 tablespoon rum or vanilla

Resift flour twice with baking powder and salt. Melt chocolate and butter over hot water. When cool, beat eggs in, one at a time. Beat in honey and flavoring. Stir in sifted ingredients. Pour batter into buttered 8 x 8-inch pan. Bake the brownies in moderate oven (375°F) for about 35 minutes.

Flavor is improved by freezing in airtight container.

CZECHOSLOVAKIAN PERNIKY
HONEY COOKIES
[start 1 day ahead]

4 cups flour
½ pound honey
1 cup granulated sugar
3 ounces each citron, lemon,
    orange peel
¼ teaspoon allspice
½ teaspoon nutmeg
1 teaspoon cinnamon

1 egg
3 to 5 tablespoons milk
3 tablespoons butter
1 teaspoon baking soda
¼ teaspoon mace
½ teaspoon cloves
rind of 1 lemon and 1 orange

Mix all ingredients well. Let stand 10 to 12 hours. Roll to ½-inch thickness. Cut out forms with cookie-cutters. Brush tops with egg white and place half of a blanched almond in center of each. Place on buttered cookie-sheet and bake in moderate oven until light-brown. When cool, ice the underside of the cookie with Lemon Icing (see index).

Note: These cookies are better 2 weeks after they are baked. They keep very well. The true honey-lover may omit the icing as it is a bit of fancying up which detracts rather than adds to the honey flavor.

CZECHOSLOVAKIAN CHOCOLATE HONEY
CAKE PERNIK

3 cups sifted flour
1¼ cups warm honey
½ cup confectioner's (pow-
    dered) sugar
¼ cup chopped almonds

1 tablespoon cocoa
1 egg, beaten
⅛ teaspoon baking soda
1 teaspoon vanilla

Sift dry ingredients 3 times. Combine with beaten egg and work into a smooth dough. Set aside for 2 hours. Roll to about ½-inch thickness, cut into shapes, and place on buttered baking-sheet. Brush with egg and bake in a hot oven, being careful not to open oven door during baking, to prevent tops from cracking. When done, decorate with Lemon Icing (see index).

Flavor improves by freezing in airtight container.

Will keep in regular cookie jar between layers of waxed paper.

EGGLESS CHRISTMAS COOKIES

½ cup honey
½ cup butter
2 cups flour

½ teaspoon cinnamon
½ teaspoon cloves
1 teaspoon baking soda

Warm honey and butter carefully for a minute or two. When cool, add dry ingredients that have been sifted together several times. Roll out to ¼ inch and cut with a doughnut cutter. Bake on buttered cookie-sheet for 12 to 15 minutes in a moderate oven (350°F). When cold, frost with confectioner's (powdered) sugar frosting. Decorate with clusters of red cinnamon candies and bits of green gumdrops to form holly-wreath design.

Makes about 24 cookies.

HONEY SOUR CREAM COOKIES

1 cup brown sugar, packed	1 egg
½ cup granulated sugar	1 teaspoon vanilla
½ cup butter	1 teaspoon baking soda
¼ teaspoon salt	½ cup sour cream
½ cup clover honey	3½ cups flour

Dissolve baking soda in sour cream. Mix all ingredients by hand and drop in walnut-size balls on greased cookie-pan, leaving room for expansion. Bake in moderate oven (350°F) for 20 minutes. Remove to a rack.

Makes 36 macaroon type cookies.

The cookies improve after standing a few days.

HONEY FRUIT BARS

½ cup butter	¼ teaspoon ground cinnamon
½ cup granulated sugar	
1 cup clover honey	¼ teaspoon ground ginger
1 well-beaten egg	½ cup sour milk
2¾ cups cake flour	¼ cup grated coconut
1 teaspoon baking soda	½ cup seedless raisins, soaked
1 teaspoon salt	until plump in hot water
¼ teaspoon ground cloves	1 cup ground walnut meats

Cream butter until soft and smooth; gradually add granulated sugar; continue creaming until mixture is light and sugar thoroughly blended, then stir in honey alternately with beaten egg. Sift flour once, measure, and sift again with baking soda, salt, cloves, cinnamon, and ginger. Stir into butter-honey mixture, alternately with sour milk. Add coconut, drained raisins, and ground walnut meats. Mix well, spread the batter to about ¼ inch on a generously buttered cookie-sheet or a shallow pan, and bake in a moderate oven (350°F) for 20 minutes. Cool to lukewarm, then cut into 3 x 1-inch strips.

Makes 24 bars.

Pack in tight fitting closed container, between layers of waxed paper, and store in a cool, dry place. Bars improve by freezing.

FRENCH COBBLESTONES

[petits-fours]

1½ cups honey	⅛ cup heated brandy
½ pound granulated sugar	1½ pounds cake flour
1 teaspoon ground cinnamon	¼ teaspoon salt
½ teaspoon ground cloves	½ teaspoon baking soda
2 teaspoons double-acting baking powder	6 tablespoons sweet butter

Boil honey together with granulated sugar for 3 or 4 minutes, or until sugar is dissolved and the two well blended; stir in cinnamon and cloves. Remove from heat and stir in heated brandy. Sift flour, salt, baking soda, and baking powder into a bowl; make a well in center and pour in the cooled honey-brandy mixture and sweet butter, then work thoroughly to a smooth dough. Roll out thinly on a slightly floured board, lay neatly and evenly on a buttered baking-sheet, and bake in a moderately hot oven (325°–350°F) until delicately browned. Cut while still hot into squares; cool and when cold, ice one portion of the petits-fours with vanilla icing, another with chocolate icing, and the remainder with orange icing.

Candied citron, pineapple, orange, or lemon peel, all finely chopped, may be added to the dough before baking.

Store in refrigerator, in airtight container, between waxed paper. Will keep a week.

ICING FOR PETITS-FOURS

2 egg whites
1½ cups confectioner's (pow-
    dered) sugar

1 teaspoon lemon juice
⅛ teaspoon cream of tartar

Beat egg whites until just frothy. Add sugar, one spoonful at a time, until blended. Add lemon juice and cream of tartar. Use any food coloring desired in part or all of the mixture.

Note: If kept white, substitute vanilla extract for lemon juice. For green, substitute pistachio extract.

COFFEE HONEY COOKIES

½ cup butter
¼ cup granulated sugar
¾ cup honey
1 egg beaten with
¼ teaspoon salt
2 cups cake flour

1½ teaspoons baking powder
¼ teaspoon baking soda
¾ teaspoon instant coffee
grated rind of 1 orange
1 teaspoon vanilla
1 cup broken nutmeats

Cream butter and sugar. Add honey and mix. Add egg and salt. Sift together twice flour, baking powder, baking soda, and instant coffee. Add to first mixture, blending quickly but thoroughly. Fold in grated rind of orange, vanilla, and nuts. Bake at 350°F for 12 to 15 minutes until edges are light golden-brown. Dry on cake racks before storing.

Makes approximately 3 dozen cookies.

They keep well and taste even better a few days after baking.

APPLESAUCE HONEY SQUARES

3 tablespoons butter	1 teaspoon double-acting
½ cup granulated sugar	baking powder
¾ cup honey	1 teaspoon baking soda
3 eggs, beaten	grated rind of 1 orange
¼ teaspoon salt	½ cup applesauce
2 cups cake flour	1 cup broken nutmeats

Cream butter and sugar; add honey; add eggs beaten with salt. Fold in flour, baking powder, and baking soda sifted together. Add rind of orange, applesauce, and nutmeats. Pour into buttered 10 x 15-inch pan and bake at 325°F 45 to 50 minutes. Cut into squares when cold.

Makes 15 or 16 large squares.

HONEY DROP CAKES

1 cup granulated sugar	½ teaspoon vanilla
½ cup butter	1½ cups sifted flour
2 tablespoons honey	2 teaspoons double-acting
¼ teaspoon salt	baking powder
2 eggs	nut meats

Beat butter. Add sifted sugar gradually and blend these ingredients until they are very light and fluffy. Add honey and salt. Beat in eggs one at a time. Add vanilla. Resift flour with baking powder. Stir sifted ingredients into butter mixture. Drop batter—1/2 teaspoon at a time—2 inches apart on a buttered sheet. Garnish each cookie with a nut meat. Bake cookies in a hot oven (400°F) for about 12 minutes.

Makes about 65 soft, chewy 2-inch cookies.

BRUSSELS COOKIES

4 cups all-purpose flour
2 teaspoons honey
1 cup brown sugar, packed
2 cups sweet butter, melted

1 egg, whole
1 teaspoon baking soda
1 teaspoon cinnamon

Mix all ingredients in electric mixer for 5 minutes, or beat for 15 minutes. Make a roll and keep in refrigerator several hours. Cut in thin slices and bake in medium oven, 350°F, until done —12 minutes.

Makes about 60 cookies.

Store in airtight container.

HONEY NUT TURNOVERS

1 pound sweet butter
1 cup sour cream
2 egg yolks

2 cups flour
1/2 teaspoon salt

Mix ingredients. Shape into small balls and place in refrigerator until cold. Roll out between sheets of waxed paper.

Spread filling (below) on half of each pastry. Fold second half over filling. Brush jointure with water and seal edges. Bake in moderate oven (350°F) for 12 minutes, or until done.

FILLING

1 teaspoon chopped nuts   1 teaspoon honey
1 teaspoon granulated sugar

Mix together, spread on pastry.
    Store in refrigerator in airtight container or freeze.

MAZEVOZKY PRIANIKI

[Russian rye honey cookies]

2 cups honey   1 cup sifted cake flour
1 cup rye flour

Heat honey in saucepan until thin. Mix rye flour and cake flour and heat in separate pan, shaking constantly so it does not change color. Remove honey from heat. Add flour mixture to it gradually, beating constantly. Continue beating with large spoon until dough comes off it easily. Shape as desired and cut with round cutter. Bake in moderate oven (350°F) on buttered sheet until well browned. They will keep indefinitely.

Note: This is a stiff, chewy, flat cookie with excellent flavor—wonderful for children.

FRENCH GÂTEAUX AU MIEL

[honey cakes]

2 eggs, well beaten   ¼ cup honey
½ cup granulated sugar   1 cup sifted flour

To the beaten eggs add sugar and honey, blending well. Gradually add flour. The batter should be semi-liquid. Let it stand
45 minutes before spreading it on a buttered cookie-sheet.
Bake for about 20 minutes in a preheated moderate oven
(350°F). Cut in squares and place them on a cake rack to cool
and harden. Keep in airtight container.
    Makes eight 2 x 2-inch squares.

LEMON HONEY SLICES

[start a day ahead]

2½ cups sifted flour   1 egg
1 teaspoon double-acting   ¼ cup honey
    baking powder   1 tablespoon grated lemon
½ teaspoon salt   rind
½ cup butter   1 tablespoon lemon juice
½ cup sugar   sugar

Sift flour, baking powder, and salt together. Blend butter and
sugar together. Cream well. Add 1 unbeaten egg, honey,
lemon rind, and lemon juice. Beat well. Blend in dry ingredients gradually. Place on waxed paper and shape into roll
1½ inches in diameter. Wrap in waxed paper. Chill over-

night, or place in freezer for several hours. Cut into slices
⅛ inch thick and place on buttered baking-sheets. Sprinkle
with sugar. Bake in moderately hot oven (400°F) 8 to 10 minutes until lightly browned. Store in tightly covered container.
Makes 6 dozen cookies.

ITALIAN FRIED COOKIES

6 eggs
¾ cup granulated sugar
3 teaspoons double-acting
   baking powder

1 teaspoon salt
5 cups stone-ground flour
¼ cup salad oil

FILLING

1 cup canned or cooked
   chick-peas, puréed
1 cup (⅓ pound) grated
   sweet chocolate
¼ cup honey
1 tablespoon finely minced
   citron

⅓ cup finely chopped wal-
   nuts
2 teaspoons grated orange
   peel
2 cups honey
2 cups chopped walnuts

Beat eggs until fluffy. Sift sugar, baking powder, salt, and flour
together and stir into eggs. Mix in salad oil. Cover and reserve
while preparing the filling. To make the latter mix chick-peas
with grated chocolate, honey, minced citron, walnuts, and
orange peel. Roll out pastry into a rectangular shape, ⅛ inch
in thickness. Divide rectangle in half. On one half, mark
2-inch squares. Place ½ teaspoon of the filling in the center of
each square. Fold the other half of the dough over and cover
the filling well. Cut into squares with a pastry edger. Press
edges together to seal. Make sure that no air is left in the

squares. Fry in deep fat, approximately 350°F, until brown, cooking no more than 4 at one time. Watch them. When brown, drain on absorbent paper. When cookies are fried, bring honey to a boil, then turn the heat very low. Dip cookies in honey, coating on all sides, then roll in finely chopped walnuts.

Makes 9 dozen.

Store between layers of waxed paper in airtight container. These cookies will keep for 2 weeks. They can be frozen indefinitely.

Note: The beans add no flavor to these cookies—they merely act as a filler for the chocolate and prevent it from seeping through the cookie dough during the frying.

CHRISTMAS CHOCOLATE BARS

2¾ cups brown sugar, packed   ½ teaspoon allspice
5 eggs   1 teaspoon baking soda
4 ounces chocolate   ½ cup honey
3 cups all-purpose flour   1 cup citron
1 tablespoon cinnamon   ½ to 1 pound almonds,
1½ teaspoons cloves   blanched and shredded

Beat eggs until light and add sifted brown sugar gradually, beating these ingredients until they are well blended. Grate and add chocolate. Combine and sift flour, cinnamon, cloves, allspice, and soda. Add the sifted ingredients to the egg mixture alternately with honey. Chop and add citron and almonds. Spread dough with a spatula in two 9 x 13-inch pans lined with waxed paper. Bake in a moderate oven (350°F). When cake is cold, ice it with Chocolate Butter Icing (see index). Cut into bars. When cold, store in container between layers of waxed paper.

CHOCOLATE BUTTER ICING

2 ounces chocolate
2 to 3 tablespoons butter
¼ cup hot water, or cream,
   or coffee

⅛ teaspoon salt
1 teaspoon vanilla
2 cups confectioner's (powdered) sugar

Melt chocolate over a very low flame. Add and melt butter.
Add hot water, cream or coffee, and salt. Remove these ingredients from the fire. When they are cool, add vanilla. Sift and
add gradually confectioner's sugar. Slightly less sugar than
given above may be required. Stir icing until it is a good
consistency to spread.

CHRISTMAS CHOCOLATE HONEY RINGS

1 cup butter
1 cup honey
2 cups flour
1 teaspoon baking soda
2 tablespoons grated
   blanched almonds
4 egg yolks

¾ cup grated sweet choco-
   late, loose
1 teaspoon grated lemon rind
1 teaspoon cinnamon
1 egg white, slightly beaten
green, or red, seed sugar

Work all ingredients, except egg white, to a smooth and soft
dough with the hands. When well blended, roll out to ⅛-inch
thickness on waxed paper and cut out with a floured ring cutter. Place rings on buttered baking-sheet. Brush with beaten
egg white. Sprinkle with green or red colored sugar. Bake in
moderate oven (350°F) for 10 to 15 minutes.

HONEY PECAN BUTTER BALLS

½ cup butter
2 tablespoons honey
1 cup flour, sifted
½ teaspoon salt
1 teaspoon vanilla

1 cup finely chopped pecan
   nutmeats
confectioner's (powdered)
   sugar

Work butter until creamy, stirring honey in gradually. Add remaining ingredients and mix thoroughly. Chill 1 hour. Then form into balls the size of small walnuts. Place well apart on buttered baking-sheets and bake in a slow oven, 300°F, about 40 minutes, or until delicately brown. Roll at once in sugar. Let cool and roll again in sugar.
    Makes 24 butterballs.
    Store between layers of waxed paper in airtight container. Freeze to keep longer than 2 weeks.

BELGIAN BERNARDINS

½ teaspoon double-acting
   baking powder
2 cups all-purpose flour sifted
½ cup brown sugar
½ cup honey, dark

¼ cup grated unbleached almonds
1 stick butter, soft
1 egg, beaten
½ cup rum

Mix all ingredients together in a bowl. Work the paste with the fingers. Let it rise for 15 minutes. Roll batter into a sausage and cool in refrigerator. Slice to ⅛ of an inch. Bake on buttered cookie-sheet, 3 inches apart, at 350°F, until brown.
    The Bernardins keep indefinitely in an airtight container. *Note:* As a Christmas special, I roll batter sausage in sugar confetti before slicing.

DUTCH KNAPKOECKEN

1 teaspoon double-acting
  baking powder, sifted
  with
2 cups flour
1 stick butter
1½ cups dark-brown sugar,
  packed

½ cup plus 2 tablespoons
  milk
¼ cup honey
1 teaspoon vanilla
milk
granulated sugar

Mix all ingredients, except milk and sugar, together in a bowl and make a smooth paste. Roll out to ⅛ of an inch. Cut into large round cookies (5 inches). Brush with cold milk and sprinkle with granulated sugar. Bake in a moderate oven (350°F) until light-brown.

Store in airtight container or freeze if necessary to keep longer than 2 weeks.

HONEY POPPY-SEED COOKIES

2 cups flour, sifted
1 tablespoon granulated
  sugar
4 eggs, slightly beaten

2 tablespoons vegetable oil
2 cups honey
¼ pound poppy seed

Mix together flour, sugar, eggs, and vegetable oil. Knead until smooth, about 5 minutes. Roll out to ¼ inch on a lightly floured board. Cut into 2-inch squares. Fold over into triangles and prick tops with a fork. Bake on a greased cookie sheet in moderate oven (350°F) until lightly browned, about 15 minutes. Drop cookies into boiling honey, stirring constantly. After 3 minutes add poppy seed. Stir constantly and cook until a rich brown. Sprinkle with 2 tablespoons cold water, stir well, and remove from heat. Place on a greased platter. Separate cookies with wet hands. Chill.

Makes 4 dozen.

Store between layers of waxed paper. Do not keep over a week.

GINGERSNAPS

2 cups sifted all-purpose flour	½ teaspoon cinnamon
¾ cup honey	½ cup dry bread crumbs
1 teaspoon baking soda	½ cup melted butter
½ teaspoon salt	2 tablespoons ice water
3 teaspoons powdered ginger	

Sift together flour, sugar, baking soda, salt, ginger, and cinnamon. Add crumbs, honey, butter, and water. Mix thoroughly. Roll ⅛ inch thick on lightly floured board or canvas. Shape with cookie-cutter. Bake on ungreased baking sheet in moderate oven (375°F) 10 minutes.

Refrigerator Ginger Snaps: Dough may be shaped in roll, wrapped in waxed paper, and stored in refrigerator. Cut chilled roll in ⅛-inch slices and bake as above.

Makes about 7 dozen 2-inch cookies.

Store in airtight container. Will keep indefinitely.

BRANDYSNAPS

½ cup honey	¼ cup butter
½ cup granulated sugar	¼ teaspoon ginger
1 cup flour	1 tablespoon brandy

Warm honey and butter. Mix thoroughly with other ingredients. Drop from teaspoon on hot cookie-sheet a few inches apart. Bake 5 minutes. Cookies spread and bubble. Shape as soon as fingers can touch them by turning cookies around handle of wooden spoon.

Cool on a rack.

Makes about 3 dozen cookies.

Note: These cookies can only be made on a dry day and must be kept in an airless container or they will get soft immediately.

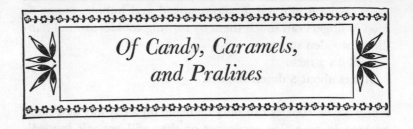

Of Candy, Caramels, and Pralines

*F*OUR thousand years ago all candy was made with honey. There is in existence an Egyptian scroll giving a recipe for a candy-type confection of honey, figs, dates, and nuts, not unlike those eaten in Algeria today. Until modern times there were but few varieties of these simple sweets. Honey gives candy a very special flavor, much different from that which sugar can provide. There is no unusual trick to learn: honey candy is as easy to make as sugar candy. Since honey confections retain all the moisture to which they are exposed, I recommend, for storage, tight-fitting cans, foil wrapping or, better still, those cans which have chemically filled moisture-absorbent knobs screwed in the lids.

I would advise everyone to use a candy thermometer. Great-grandma may have done without, but I suspect that she didn't produce anything comparable to our best store candies, except in flavor. Today we find it important for a candy to both taste and look wonderful.

To avoid breakage, place the candy thermometer in water before using and bring it to a boil to test accuracy; it should register 212°F. Make sure the bulb is fully immersed and does not touch the pan. Avoid sudden changes of temperature. Hang it up when not in use. Always use pots that are smooth on the inside. Candy dippers, marble slabs, and miniature molds which help give your candy a professional look are available in most large hardware stores.

ALGERIAN DATES

2 packages pitted dates
½ cup honey (approximately)
½ cup chopped, lightly
   toasted almonds

¼ cup candied citron
½ cup chopped walnuts
1 cup granulated sugar

Mix nutmeats, citron, and just enough honey to make them adhere. Fill dates neatly with mixture. Roll in sugar and store between layers of waxed paper in a tin can.

Note: This is a winter candy.

HONEY BITTERSWEETS

½ honey comb
hot water

2 pounds semi-sweet chocolate

Allow comb honey to remain in refrigerator 24 hours before using. Cut into pieces about ¾ inch long and ⅜ inch wide with knife that is dipped in boiling water. Place pieces on trays covered with waxed paper. Chill 30 minutes.

Meanwhile melt chocolate in top of double boiler over warm water. Stir until melted. Remove from heat and, if necessary, cool rapidly over cold water to a temperature of 70 to 75°F on candy thermometer. Have a sturdy wire—a foot long —bent like a tweezer or a regular candy dipper, hold squares between ends and dip into chocolate once, then chill. Repeat operation, taking care that the spot where tweezers touched candy at first dipping is covered by second coating of chocolate so there will be no leakage of honey.

Note: Candy dippers can be bought at, or ordered through, better hardware stores in most large cities.

RUM HONEY CARAMELS

1 cup granulated sugar   2 cups heavy cream
1 cup strained honey   1 tablespoon sweet butter
½ teaspoon cream of tartar   1 tablespoon rum
½ cup cold top milk   ½ teaspoon vanilla extract

Place in a saucepan granulated sugar, strained honey, cream of
tartar, and milk; stir to blend well, and cook over a low flame,
stirring frequently, to the hard ball stage (255°F). Gradually
stir in scalded heavy cream, watching that the mixture never
stops boiling gently and stirring constantly. Add sweet butter
and rum, mixed with vanilla extract, and cook again to the
hard ball stage. Pour at once into a buttered or oiled pan;
mark deeply in small squares when almost cold, and when
quite cold, cut and wrap each caramel in a piece of waxed
paper.
    Makes about 24 caramels.
    Store in a tightly closed tin in a cool, dry, dark place.

HONEY PENUCHE

2 cups brown sugar   ¼ cup honey
¼ teaspoon salt   3 tablespoons butter
⅔ cup white sugar   ½ cup chopped nuts
1 cup milk

Combine all ingredients except butter and nuts. Cook over
low flame to 240°F. Stir just enough to prevent sticking. Remove from fire, add butter. Cool to lukewarm. Do not stir.
When cooled, beat until candy begins to thicken. Add nuts

and turn into greased shallow pan. When firm, cut into squares.

Makes about 24 squares.

NOUGAT

[start a day ahead]

1 cup honey
6 tablespoons light corn syrup
2 cups granulated sugar
1 cup water
3 egg whites stiffly beaten

1 cup coarsely chopped
   blanched almonds
½ cup cherries
1 teaspoon almond extract

Cook first four ingredients to 265°F on the candy thermometer. Slowly add this syrup to egg whites while beating. When the mixture begins to stiffen add cherries, almonds, and almond extract. Pour into buttered cookie-sheet. Cover with waxed paper and press down with weighted metal tray. Let nougat stand overnight.

Cut into strips and wrap in waxed paper.

Note: Wafer paper should line cookie-sheet, if possible. It is obtainable at most bakers'-supply stores listed in the Classified Telephone Directory.

NOUGAT DE MONTELIMART

1 cup honey flavored with 1
   teaspoon instant coffee
   or 1 teaspoon pistachio
   or 1 teaspoon vanilla
   or 1 teaspoon frozen

orange juice
2 egg whites, beaten very
   stiffly
3 cups blanched, slivered,
   lightly toasted almonds

Rub a cookie-sheet with corn oil. Line cookie-sheet with wafer paper. Reserve. Bring honey to soft crack stage, just over

260°F on candy thermometer. Add egg whites. Then bring honey back to soft crack stage and add almonds. Pour quickly and evenly on cookie-sheet. Cover with another sheet of wafer paper and cut in 2 x 1-inch rectangles while still warm. Cool. Wrap each rectangle in waxed paper. Will keep indefinitely.

Note: Wafer paper can be obtained from most bakers' suppliers listed in the Classified Telephone Directory.

CHOCOLATE TORRONE

½ cup honey
1 cup granulated sugar
2 tablespoons water
2 egg whites
1¾ cups cocoa
2 tablespoons water

1 tablespoon granulated sugar
1¼ pounds shelled hazelnuts or almonds lightly toasted

Place honey in top of double boiler over boiling water; stir constantly until honey is caramelized. Combine sugar and water in small saucepan and let boil until caramelized. Beat egg whites until stiff and add to honey a little at a time, mixing well. Add sugar and mix well. Combine cocoa with 2 tablespoons water and 1 tablespoon sugar and cook until creamy. Mix with first mixture. Line two or three 6 x 8-inch loaf-pans with wafer paper and pour in mixture about 2 inches deep. Allow to cool, then cut into 2 long pieces from each pan. Wrap in waxed paper.
    Keeps indefinitely.

IMBERLACH FOR THE JEWISH SEDER FESTIVAL

1¼ cups honey   ½ teaspoon ginger
2 cups granulated sugar   ½ teaspoon cinnamon
1 cup water   2 cups chopped nuts
⅛ teaspoon salt   4 cups matzoth farfel

Cook honey, sugar, and water in a large saucepan over low heat 5 minutes, but do not stir until candy thermometer registers 255°F. Remove from heat and stir in salt, spices, nuts, and farfel. Pour onto greased cookie-sheet or platter and flatten out until about ½ inch thick. Cool and cut into squares or diamonds.

Note: Matzoth farfel can be bought around Passover (Easter) at any kosher delicatessen.

HONEY MARSHMALLOWS

1 tablespoon gelatin   1 cup honey
¼ cup cold water   ¾ to 1 pound coconut

Soak gelatin well in cold water. Dissolve gelatin over hot water and add to the honey which has been warmed. Beat until very light and fluffy (about 10 minutes in blender, and 20 minutes by hand). Turn out on buttered pan and let stand 24 to 48 hours. Dip knife into cold water and cut into squares. Toast coconut and roll to make fine. Roll each piece in the coconut.
    Store in airtight container.

HONEY TAFFY

2 cups granulated sugar   ⅔ cup cold water
2 cups honey   ⅛ teaspoon salt

Boil sugar, honey, and water to brittle stage, 288°F on candy
thermometer. Add salt. Stir only enough to prevent burning.
Put in buttered dish to cool; pull as soon as you can handle.
When pulling, dip hands frequently in cold water. Pull until
white. Wrap individually in waxed paper.

HONEY DIVINITY

2 cups granulated sugar   2 egg whites
⅓ cup honey   ½ cup chopped nut meats
⅓ cup water

Boil sugar, honey, and water until syrup spins a thread, 278°F.
Pour syrup over well-beaten egg whites, beating continuously.
Just before mixture starts to set, add chopped nut meats.
When mixture crystallizes, drop with a spoon on waxed paper.

Note: Candied cherries or candied rhubarb may be added.

HONEY FUDGE

2 cups granulated sugar   1 cup evaporated milk
4 ounces unsweetened choco-   ¼ cup honey
     late   2 tablespoons butter
¼ teaspoon salt   1 cup nuts

Boil sugar, chocolate, salt, and milk for 5 minutes. Add honey and cook to soft-ball stage, 240°F. Add butter; let stand until lukewarm; beat until creamy, add nuts, and pour into buttered pan. Cut when firm.

GREEK HALVA

3 cups farina	¼ pound chopped almonds
1 cup olive oil	½ teaspoon each of pow-
1 cup honey	dered clove and cinna-
1 cup water	mon
2 cups granulated sugar	powdered sugar or cinnamon

Heat oil until very hot. Pour farina into it gradually and stir slowly until farina browns (30 to 45 minutes). Make a syrup in the meantime by boiling sugar, water, and honey for ½ hour. Add clove, cinnamon, and nuts. Stir constantly over slow fire until mass thickens. Cover pan 5 minutes. Pour out on oiled cookie-sheet and cut into squares when cool. Sprinkle with powdered sugar or cinnamon.

BONBONS

2 cups granulated sugar	2 egg whites, beaten until
1 cup water	frothy
½ cup honey	¼ cup chopped nuts, coarse
12 marshmallows	¼ cup candied fruit

Make a syrup of sugar, water, and honey and boil without disturbing to hard-ball stage, 245°F. In the meantime cut up 12 marshmallows, using knife dipped in powdered sugar, and drop slices in syrup. As they melt, stir thoroughly and when blended, beat in the egg whites. Pour into buttered pan. As mass stiffens, quickly press in the nuts and fruit. Cut into small fancy shapes.

Note: Small fancy cutters can be bought at better hardware stores everywhere.

PENNIES FROM HEAVEN

½ cup water   1 cup orange blossom honey

Heat honey, bring to a boil and continue boiling to 240°F on the candy thermometer. Then drop, one teaspoon at a time, into a pan full of firmly packed cracked ice.

The candies are hard and flat. It takes a little practice to make them round.

Wrap individually in waxed paper for storage.

Note: We used to make them with snow on winter afternoons at my grandmother's.

MY OWN PRALINES

2 cups praline powder (see   4 tablespoons cocoa mixed
    index)   with 1 teaspoon cinna-
8 ounces semi-sweet chocolate   mon

Melt chocolate over boiling water in top of double boiler. Mix in praline powder. Cool a little. Shape into balls the size of a hazelnut. Roll in cocoa-cinnamon mixture and place on sheet of waxed paper in cool spot to harden. Keep between layers of waxed paper in tin box.

Makes about 40 pralines.

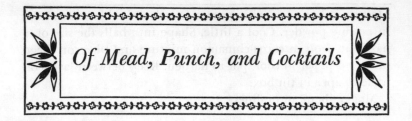

Of Mead, Punch, and Cocktails

FERMENTED beverages with a honey base appear in the history of most nations. Until the grapevine was introduced from China to the Mediterranean shores, the Northern countries only knew mead, the simplest of all alcoholic drinks. There are many forms of mead: Nordic legends represent the gods drinking it from horns, as the East Africans drink their honeyed *tetsch* today. Attila's men quaffed *kvas* or *koumis* according to the season. The Britons, well before Roman times, kept themselves happy on huge quantities of mead, while the Celts went one step further and made a distillation of it which they used during the ritual ceremonies accompanying Druidic sacrifices. The Tibetan monks spike theirs with rice brandy to make the most potent drink in the world, and the Koreans run a good second with their *Misshu*.

Through the ages, divines and quacks have used honey in their potions. To this day, Zulu witches of the African veld make a magic drink from fermented honeycombs and a severed human foot. In gentler civilizations honey and wine were often used, together with spices and poppy juice, to induce erotic dreams or boost failing strength. Greek Olympic runners drank a sour wine mixed with honey and salt. Henry IV of France was said to have restored his youthful potency every night with a *coulis,* a kind of double-strength consommé made from six partridges, six egg yolks, six tablespoons of honey, ground cinnamon, and one cup of Jurançon wine. This nightcap is supposed to have earned him the title of *"Vert Gallant."*

Many a Saxon thane died prematurely from an intemperate addiction to mead. Loving the taste of honey too well, those Britons might have found a consolation in the story of Alexander the Great; he proved that you can take it with you. He was buried standing upright in a jar of honey and, accidentally, became a perfect mummy. Such mummies became greatly sought after by ancient Persians, who attributed miraculous healing power to them. Despite the fact that only a small piece of mummy was carried around as an amulet, the supply became entirely inadequate, and a mummy black market developed. A manuscript of that period describes the procedure for making fake ones: "Find a ruddy, red-haired manchild—feed it on fruit till it is 30 years old. Drown it in a stone vessel filled with honey. Seal it and do not open for 150 years. . . ." A long-term investment for something which soon went out of style!

MEAD

4 quarts water	2 tablespoons lemon juice
2 cups honey	1 teaspoon powdered cloves
½ cup brown sugar	1 teaspoon powdered ginger
2 egg whites, beaten	½ envelope yeast, diluted
1 tablespoon grated lemon	with
peel	1 tablespoon lukewarm water

Heat and mix honey, water, and sugar. Add egg whites and simmer until sugar is melted. Skim. Cool. Add spices, grated lemon peel and juice, and yeast. Allow to stand in large kettle or crock until it stops working (several days). Bottle and cork. Securely fasten cork with wire. Stand, cork down, like champagne, and turn bottles from time to time. Drink after 6 months.

Note: Imported bottled mead from Denmark is available here at some liquor stores.

OULD MAN'S MILK

1 bottle ale	¼ teaspoon ginger
¼ teaspoon powdered cinna-	2 egg yolks
mon	1 scant teaspoon honey
¼ teaspoon nutmeg	2 jiggers Scotch

Heat ale in saucepan. Dust with spices. Beat eggs with honey until light and frothy. Just before ale comes to a boil, pour egg mixture into it, stirring it with a whisk. Just before drinking, add Scotch and stir. Drink hot.
Serves 1.

LOUIS XIV HYPOCRAS

1 quart of good claret
½ cup honey, warm
¼ teaspoon cinnamon
¼ teaspoon cayenne pepper
¼ teaspoon powdered ginger

¼ teaspoon mace
12 cloves
½ teaspoon almond extract
1 russet apple, sliced

Blend honey into claret until it does not settle to the bottom anymore. Add all other ingredients. Allow to stand overnight. Strain twice through 4 thicknesses of cheesecloth. Bottle and cork tightly.

Keeps indefinitely.

Note: The good burghers of Paris used to send this to their king, who liked it very much.

HYDROMEL

4 quarts of water
2 cups honey

1 cup brandy

Boil water and honey until syrup is reduced by half. Skim carefully. Cool. Add brandy. Bottle and cork.

Keeps 10 to 12 years.

TARTAR KVAS

3 pounds hardened pumpernickel bread
18 quarts boiling water
4 cups honey

1½ packages dry yeast
1 tablespoon flour
raisins

Place bread in a five-gallon barrel. Add boiling water. Cover and allow to cool until lukewarm. Filter through a cloth without pressing the mixture. Add honey previously mixed with dry yeast and flour. Pour strained liquid into empty keg. Allow to stand for 12 hours at room temperature. Then strain again and fill bottles with raisins and liquid. Cork and keep in a cool place for 2 days. Drink well chilled.

TURKISH KOUMIS

¼ cup flour, mixed with   1 package dry yeast
1 quart milk   separately 3 quarts milk
1 cup honey

Allow to stand 24 hours, then add 3 more quarts milk. Drink ice cold.

Note: Sheep's, donkey's, or cow's milk may be used. Contains alcohol.

MULLED WINE

4 cups claret (red wine)   2 sticks cinnamon
2 cups water   2 cups honey
1 thinly sliced lemon   2 teaspoons poppyseed (op-
6 cloves   tional)
4 berries allspice

Boil all together for a few seconds. Drink piping hot.
    Serves 4.
Note: This drink is derived from the "Mulsum of Ancient Ro-

mans" and is still favored in many households in France, England, and Belgium.

STEWED QUAKER

1 cup West Indian molasses 1 cup honey
1 teaspoon powdered ginger juice of 2 lemons
¼ pound fresh butter

Put molasses, honey, ginger, and butter in a saucepan. Set it over the heat and simmer slowly for ½ hour, stirring frequently. Do not boil. Mix in lemon juice. Cover pan and allow to simmer 5 minutes longer. Drink hot, at once.
Serves 2.

Note: To get the Quaker properly stewed, I suggest you add a generous jigger of bourbon.

CLAIRENE AU MIEL FROM HAITI

2 teaspoons strained honey 1½ jiggers white rum

Dissolve honey in rum. Pour over ¼ cup cracked ice in martini mixer. Strain into glasses.
Serves 1.

BEES' KNEES

1 jigger honey 1 jigger lemon juice
1 jigger gin

Pour over ice. Shake. Strain into glasses.
Serves 1.

FLAMING YOUTH COCKTAIL

[from New Orleans]

1 jigger honey   3 jiggers gin
2 jiggers cream

Pour over ice. Shake. Strain into glasses.
Serves 1.

ATHOL BROSE

1 jigger top milk or cream   2 jiggers 10-year-old Scotch
1 jigger clear honey

Mix hot milk and honey. Cool. Pour over ice. Add Scotch.
Strain into glasses.
Serves 2.

HONEY BAR SYRUP

4 cups honey   1 egg white, well beaten
1 cup water

Heat and dissolve honey in water. Stir in egg white. Boil up
briskly and when the scum rises, skim carefully. Bottle for use
in cold drinks and punches.
Note: Though highly unorthodox, I have used ½ teaspoonful
of this syrup per glass in a French Seventy-five, which is a Tom
Collins with champagne instead of soda.

EIGHTEENTH-CENTURY SYLLABUB

Dilute 1 cup honey in ½ cup of hot cider. Pour into basin.
Add cold cider to make a quart. Grate in some nutmeg, then
hold it under the cow and milk into it till it has fine froth on
top. Strew over it a handful of currants, cleaned, washed, and
picked and plumped before the fire.

MODERN VERSION OF SYLLABUB

1 cup honey	cold cider to make a quart of
½ cup cider, hot	the syllabub
½ can evaporated milk,	1 teaspoon nutmeg
chilled thoroughly	½ cup raisins, soaked until
	plump

Dilute honey in cider. Pour in basin, add cold cider and nutmeg. Beat canned milk till frothy and pour into basin. Garnish with soaked-until-plump raisins.

LEMON HONEYADE

1 lemon	1 cup water
1 to 3 tablespoons honey	ice

Squeeze lemon. Add honey to juice. Stir to dissolve and add
water. Serve over ice in large glasses. Garnish with lemon slice
on rim. Add a cherry or mint sprig for color.
  Serves 1.

ORANGE HONEYADE

2 cups orange juice   ½ cup honey
½ cup lemon juice   1 cup water

Combine ingredients and stir well to dissolve honey. Pour over cracked ice in tall glasses. Garnish with orange slices, mint sprigs, and berries or cherries.
  Serves 4.

APRICOT NECTAR

½ cup orange juice   3 tablespoons honey
¼ cup soaked dried apricots

Blend for 30 seconds in electric blender.
  Serves 1.

HOT MULLED PUNCH

5 (No. 2) cans apple juice   2 (46-ounce) cans grapefruit-
3 (2-inch) sticks cinnamon   orange-juice blend
1 tablespoon nutmeg   2 oranges
6 pints cranberry juice   1 lemon
1½ cups honey   whole cloves
                                    1 quart Grand Marnier or
                                        Cointreau (optional)

Pour apple juice into kettle, add cinnamon and nutmeg, and simmer for 20 minutes. Add cranberry juice cocktail and grapefruit-orange-juice blend. Stud oranges and lemon with cloves; drop into punch and heat to boiling. Stir in honey. Heat punch bowl and fill with heated liquid and spiced fruit.

Makes approximately 2 gallons punch—or 2 cups each for 50 people.

GOGL-MOGL

2 egg yolks   1 cup milk
½ cup honey

Beat egg yolks and honey until thick, frothy, and almost white. Bring milk to boiling point. Mix and drink at the onset of a cold.

Serves 1.

SPICED FRUIT PUNCH

2½ cups orange juice
1 cup canned pineapple juice
2 cups cold water
½ cup confectioner's (powdered) sugar
2 tablespoons grated lemon rind
1 quart your favorite white wine or champagne (optional)
1 tablespoon honey
6 whole cloves
½ teaspoon nutmeg
½ teaspoon cinnamon
6 cups ginger ale
crushed ice

Combine all ingredients except ginger ale and ice. Let chill for at least 3 hours. Strain. Add ginger ale and ice.

Makes about 4 quarts before adding ice.

HONEY CHOCOLATE

8 tablespoons honey   4 cups bottled milk or
6 tablespoons chocolate-   2 cups evaporated milk and
   flavored malt drink   2 cups water
4 eggs, separated

Simmer honey and chocolate-flavored malt drink together for
2 minutes, or until syrupy, stirring constantly. Beat egg yolks,
add milk and 4 tablespoons of the honey mixture. Beat until
thoroughly combined, then chill. Just before serving, beat egg
whites until stiff, then add remaining honey mixture, while
continuing to beat. Place a spoonful of the egg-white mixture
in each of 4 tall glasses, then fill each glass ⅔ full of the milk
mixture, and top with another spoonful of the egg-white mixture.

Serves 4.

CHILDREN'S PARTY DRINK

1 quart currants or raisins   the juice of 5 oranges
1 pint water   the juice of 3 lemons
1 cup honey   water
1 small stick cinnamon

Wash currants, place in a kettle, and cover with water. Reserve
¼ cup currants for garnishing. Simmer gently for 10 minutes.
Strain. If a clear juice is desired, do not press the pulp. Combine the pint of water, honey, and cinnamon and boil for 5
minutes. Remove the spice stick. Combine the juice of the
oranges, lemons, and the currant juice with the spiced syrup,

diluted to taste. Fresh pineapple or cranberry juice may be used instead of orange and lemon juice. Serve hot or cold.

Makes about 2 quarts.

REMEDY AGAINST HOARSENESS

½ pint strained honey   1 tablespoon salad oil
juice of 1 lemon

Blend together in the mixer.
Serves 1.

PHYSICAL AND CHEMICAL PROPERTIES OF EXTRACTED (LIQUID) HONEY OF AVERAGE COMPOSITION

The Average Chemical Composition of American Honey

[Based on a sample of 500 milliliters (1.057 pints) of "average" extracted honey, at 68°F (20°C.), total weight 708 grams (25.0 oz. avoirdupois)]

THE PRINCIPAL COMPONENTS [1]

		(Percent)	(Grams)
Water (natural moisture)		17.70	125
Levulose (d-fructose; fruit sugar)	40.50		287
Dextrose (d-glucose; grape sugar)	34.02		241
Sucrose (granulated, cane or beet sugar)	1.90		13
Total Sugars		76.42	541
Dextrin (including gum-like substances)		1.51	11
Ash (mineral substances; potash, soda, lime, magnesia, chlorides, sulphates, phosphates, silica, iron, manganese, copper)		0.18	1
Total		95.81	678

[1] Representing the average of the analyses of 92 samples of honey, **by** Dr. Charles A. Browne (U.S. Bur. of Chemistry Bulletin 110, now out **or** print)

SUBSTANCES OCCURRING IN RELATIVELY SMALL QUANTITIES

Acids (Formic, Acetic, Malic, Citric, Succinic, Amino Acids. Total free acid, calculated as Formic acid 0.08%; 0.6 g.)
Pollen grains; particles of beeswax

From. U.S. Department of Agriculture, Bulletin, March 15, 1946

Albuminoids (proteins)
Maltose and less common sugars (sometimes Melezitose)
Pigments (Carotin, Chlorophyll and Chlorophyll derivatives,
    Xanthophyll)
Substances usually present, but for which the quantitative
    determination is difficult:
  Flavors and Aromatic substances (Terpenes, Aldehydes, Esters)
  Higher Alcohols (Mannitol, Dulcitol)
  Tannins
  Enzymes, including Invertase (converts sucrose to dextrose
    and levulose)
  Diastase (converts starch to maltose and possibly dextrose)
  Catalase (decomposes hydrogen peroxide)
  Inulase (converts inulin to levulose)
  The B-Vitamins and Vitamin C (Ascorbic acid),
    in small amounts.

	Total	4.19	30
	Grand Total	100.00	708 Grams

PHYSICAL PROPERTIES OF AVERAGE HONEY

At a temperature of 68° Fahrenheit (20°C), the *Specific-Gravity* of average honey is 1.4191 (based on weight, in air, of an equal volume of water, at the same temperature). This density corresponds to 80.66 degrees *Brix,* or 42.79 degrees Baumé. One pound occupies a volume of 10.84 fluid ounces (320.6 milliliters). One gallon weighs 11 pounds, 12.9 ounces. The *Caloric Value* of one pound of this honey is 1,488 Calories; of 100 grams, 328 Calories; of 100 milliliters (at 68°F) 464 Calories. Average honey, of the composition shown, possesses a *Refractive Index,*—determined under standard conditions,—of 1.4922 at 68°F; or 1.4910 at 77°F (25°C). It has a *Vapor-Pressure* at 68°F corresponding to that in an atmosphere in which the Relative Humidity is approximately 60 percent, at 68°F.

COMPONENT RELATIONSHIPS

One pound (453.6 grams) of average honey measuring 10.84 fluid ounces at 68°F, contains 2.83 oz. (80.3 grams) of water, equivalent to 2.72 fluid ounces (80.5 milliliters) of water. It will be noted that the *volume* of the contained water amounts to 25.1 percent of the volume of honey, although the water content amounts to 17.7 percent on a *weight* basis. The difference is, of course, due to the relatively high specific-gravity of the honey.

Although 1 gallon of average extracted honey contains slightly more than 9 pounds of total sugars, its *sweetening power* is equivalent to approximately 11 pounds, 4 ounces of granulated sugar, because of the 25 percent greater sweetening effect attributed to the honey sugars. On the basis of measured volumes, 1 volume (e.g. 1 cupful) of the honey has approximately the same sweetening power as 1⅔ volumes (1⅔ cupfuls, in the example) of granulated sugar. On the basis of weights, 1 pound of average honey containing nearly 18 percent of water, has about the same sweetening power as 0.95 pound (15¼ ounces) of granulated sugar.

Index

A NOTE ON THE TYPE

The text of this book was set on the Linotype in a face called Baskerville, named for John Baskerville (1706–75), of Birmingham, England, who was a writing master with a special renown for cutting inscriptions in stone. About 1750 he began experimenting with punch-cutting and making typographical material, which led, in 1757, to the publication of his first work, a Virgil in royal quarto, with great primer letters, in which the types throughout had been designed by him. This was followed by his famous editions of Milton, the Bible, the Book of Common Prayer, and several Latin classic authors. His types foreshadowed what we know today as the "modern" group of type faces, and these and his printing became greatly admired. After his death Baskerville's widow sold all his punches and matrices to the SOCIÉTÉ PHILOSOPHIQUE, LITTÉRAIRE ET TYPOGRAPHIQUE (totally embodied in the person of Beaumarchais, author of THE MARRIAGE OF FIGARO and the BARBER OF SEVILLE), which used some of the types to print the seventy volume edition, at Kehl, of Voltaire's works. After a checkered career on the Continent, where they dropped out of sight for some years, the punches and matrices finally came into the possession of the distinguished Paris type-founders, Deberney & Peignot, who, in singularly generous fashion, returned them to the Cambridge University Press in 1953.